NIGHTSHADE

NEW IRISH PLAYS

NIGHTSHADE

STEWART PARKER

All professional and amateur rights in this play are strictly reserved and applications for permission to perform it must be made in advance to Marc Berlin, London Management, 235/241 Regent Street, London W1A 2JT, England.

©Stewart Parker 1980

ISBN 0 905441 30 3

First published in 1980
Co-op Books (Publishing) Ltd
50 Merrion Square, Dublin 2

Co-op Books and the Irish Writers' Co-operative exist to provide outlets for Irish writing through publications and the organisation of public readings. The assistance of An Chomhairle Ealaion (The Arts Council) in the publication of this book is gratefully acknowledged.

Special thanks to Sean McCarthy and Douglas Kennedy of the Abbey and Peacock Theatres.

Design: Brendan Foreman
Typesetting: Gifford & Craven, 50 Merrion Square, Dublin 2.
Make-up: Susanne Linde

ABBEY/PEACOCK PLAY SERIES

Introductory Note

Historically, the Abbey's fundamental commitment has been the presentation of the best of contemporary Irish writing. It has at all times sought out and made accessible that writing which best reflects the various aspects of Irish society. Today it is at once more pressing and more complex for the theatre to remain a platform for the most vital Irish writers. In this series, Co-Op Books give us four fine examples of writers whose work appears on the Abbey and Peacock stages in 1980.

Stewart Parker's work, especially *Spokesong* and *Catchpenny Twist*, is already known to many. After a spell of writing successfully for television, he makes a welcome return to the theatre with *Nightshade*. His work is a welcome challenge to any theatre because he is at all times a great innovator. His disturbing new play stretches both theatre and audience to the limits.

Like Stewart Parker, Graham Reid – author of *The Closed Door* – is from Belfast. His work concerns itself with exploring the disturbing depths of life in that city. His uncompromising questions and bleak humour place him firmly among our most important contemporary dramatists.

If there is a writer who reflects the 'New Ireland' it must be Bernard Farrell. In *Canaries* he gives us a perfect picture of the new up-and-coming Irish middle-class. His astute characterisations and theatrical flair show him as being in the best tradition of Irish comic writing.

Neil Donnelly's writing arises from the dying rural-based towns of Ireland's mid-lands. He tackles with intensity the most desperate contemporary problems. What is most admirable in *Upstarts* is that he achieves this with lyrical warmth and humour.

Dedication

For Kate, as ever.

Original Cast

Nightshade was first presented at the Peacock Theatre, Dublin on the 9th October 1980 with the following cast:

Quinn	T.P. McKENNA
Delia	LISE-ANN McLAUGHLIN
The Dean	MICHAEL DUFFY
Miss Gault	MAUREEN TOAL
Vance	COLM MEANEY
Dr. Dempster	KATE FLYNN
Albert Bell	GEOFFREY GOLDEN
Vincent Kane	NIALL O'BRIEN

The play was directed by Chris Parr and designed by Bronwen Casson. Lighting by Tony Wakefield.

Quinn, 46
Delia, his daughter, 16.
The Dean, his brother-in-law, 47.
Vance, 24.
Miss Gault, 40.
Dr. Dempster, 62.
Albert Bell, 56.
Vincent Kane, 31.
Male Employee.
Girl Employee.

ACT ONE

The place is a city within the British Isles. The time is the immediate future.

The setting is formalised and symmetrical, with the disproportion of a dream. There is a great back wall like the facade of a mausoleum, with the name JOHN QUINN carved across it. Underneath are the words MAGICIAN AND MORTICIAN (MAGICIAN is over the stage right area, and MORTICIAN over the stage left). There are heavy outer doors in the bottom corners of this wall. At its centre is a shiny black curtain, lustrously swagged and tucked, which can be drawn up to reveal what is – figuratively as well as literally – an inner stage.

Before this curtained inner stage is a broad arc of platform, the circumference of which is stepped – three steps leading down to what remains of the main-stage area. This raised platform will serve as a kind of all-purpose public room. The remaining mainstage area (which serves for various private rooms) is furnished as follows: mid-way down, on extreme left and right, there are identical steel-and-chromium office desks and chairs. To the immediate left and right of centre, hard by the platform steps, there are identical large leather reclining armchairs. The vicinity of these armchairs is Quinn's home, which is next door to his funeral parlour.

Each side wall has three identical interior doors, evenly spaced. They should be used at random, as should the outer doors in the back wall. The action is fast and continuous, a constant traffic, the fitful opening and closing of possibilities. The staging and lighting should be as magic as possible: discoveries, disappearances, transformations; one foot through the looking-glass, at least.

Darkness first. Then the curtain rises on the inner stage to reveal Quinn, in topper and tails, lighting a cigarette. Disposed about the public room and the steps, listening, are the shadowy figures of Vance, Kane, Bell, the Dean, the Male Employee and the Girl Employee, some of them holding plates and drinks.

Quinn You don't need me to tell you people. . . miracles can be made to happen. The impossible takes a little time, that's all. One year in this case. We showed them how – *(he opens his matchbox again, but this time pulls a red handkerchief out of it)* – matchless, that's the word for it. Double your fleet of motors. Triple your turnover. A new branch in the New Year, how do we do it? Business sense. Hard graft. Team work – *(he is stubbing out the cigarette on the hanky, and now holds up the hanky unmarked)* – a performance not to be sneezed at, in this day and age. With the country in rags and tatters all around us – *(he produces a soup plate)* – and plenty of other firms in the soup, as well you know. With Mr. Wolf at the door. But not round this way, friends. We're living in the modern world – *(he drapes the hanky over the soup plate)* – we're perfecting the tricks of the trade round here. And that spells growth! *(he whips the hanky away; the plate has sprouted flowers).* Expansion. An unmitigated success, in fact, and it was us together than pulled it off. You and me and nobody else. So now, a toast – *(he drapes the hanky over his left hand)* – to a great year gone by, my friends, and a better one yet ahead. Because we're only starting out, you see. This is just the warm-up. You've seen nothing yet. There'll be branches sprouting all over. Buildings out of thin air. Business like you've never seen. One fine day we'll be taking over this city – here's to it! *(He whips the hanky away to reveal a glass of wine which he sips. Applause from the others. He throws the hanky into the air and it turns into a snake. He bows)* Thank you, you're very kind. And now by way of a modest grand finale – my assistant and I have prepared a little surprise. Presto!

(Gong. Quinn hauls from the inner stage wings a tall magician's box, and opens it to reveal Delia inside, dressed in a black satin tap-dance outfit and spangled tights. Music starts off. Delia steps out, and Quinn turns the box round to show the inside empty, tapping on the inside walls. He then ushers Delia into it again, closes it up and turns it a full 360 degrees. Drum roll. Quinn takes a short plank, slots it into the side of the box, and pushes it through. Then a second and a third as the drum roll builds. He then holds up a large ornamental sword, slots it in, and pushes.

There is a frightening scream from inside. Blood spurts out and runs down the front of the box. The music stops. Quinn suddenly tears the box open in a frenzy. Delia stands inside, clutching her stomach, face contorted in pain. Music starts again, very loud. She suddenly springs out with a dazzling smile, into a quick tap routine, and dances off. The music stops, the curtain falls on the inner stage, Quinn having moved down into the public room. There is a moment's awkaward silence)

Quinn Well now, there's you cue, everybody! Time to work off all that grub, what do you say? The dance floor beckons, who's game for a stagger around?

(All except Kane and Bell move off, chatting)

Save one for me now, ladies, don't forget the old boss!

Vance *(lingering at his elbow)* I didn't know you were a magician, Mr. Quinn.

Quinn Oh, just my party piece, Vance.

Vance You do it most professionally.

Quinn Isn't she rare?

Vance Your daughter, is it?

Quinn A born comedian. Every professional man needs a recreation, Vance.

Vance Indeed.

Quinn I do the odd social evening. For the church or Masonic Lodge or that. Children's parties.

Vance Very impressive.

Quinn Simple stuff on the whole.

(Slight pause)

Vance She's a lovely girl.

Quinn A gifted child, you know. Years ahead of herself, in the brain-box.

Vance Is that so?

Quinn No credit to me, I'm afraid. She's forever trying to put one over on her old man, eh?

Vance Yes.

Quinn What about yourself?

Vance In what way?

Quinn Any hobbies?

Vance Well. Driving.

Quinn After you, Vance, go ahead.

(They go off. A band can be heard from an adjacent ballroom playing 'That Old Black Magic')

(Kane and Bell are left sitting on the steps. Pause)

Kane The first four hours are the worst.

Bell You'd wonder where he gets all the energy from.

Kane Listen, if you were coining money at the rate he is. . . you'd be sawing through ladies rings round you.

(Pause)

Bell Say what you like, Vincent – but there'll never be a go-slow in the funeral business.

Kane *(looking at the side of his right foot)* Oh Christ.

Bell What's up?

Kane I've got blood on my shoe from that motorway job.

Bell It's never even been entertained. In the whole seventy years of the union's existence.

Kane I only bought them last month.

Bell. You can dye them.

Kane This is exactly the sort of thing, you see. People need waking up. A fellow gets his face stove in on his steering wheel, and who's expected to scrape it into the plastic bag? His own mother wouldn't go near it. Let alone the other driver. We're talking about people who can barely face it when their pussy-cat pukes on the Axminster.

Bell All in a day's work.

Kane People who blench at eating rabbit pie. While we're out scooping their son's intestines back into the stomach cavity, with all due reverence and dignity, of course.

Bell All part of the job, Vincent. It's a public service.

Kane Don't talk to me about public service. We're invisible men to the public.

Bell The very idea of industrial action is just outlandish.

Kane The funeral service managements have been getting away with murder.

Bell Quinn's not the worst.

Kane It's money on the table I'm looking for.

Bell He's open to reason.

Kane We'll see. We'll see what he can pull out of the hat in real life. *(Pause. He stands up)* I must have a word with the new assistant.

Bell A slippery-looking customer.

Kane You never know, he might come in very handy, the same Vance. C'mon, we'd better join the bunfight.

Bell *(rising)* All the same, Quinn had me fooled there for a minute – with the blood coming out of the box.

Kane The daughter had *him* fooled.

Bell D'you reckon? She's a bit of a practical jester, right enough.

Kane Nutty as a fruitcake, if you want my opinion. She's a worse case than the da.

Bell Not a word of the wife, for over a year now. Isn't it mystifying?

Kane Aye, Agnes outdid the pair of them there. She was the escapologist.

(They follow the others off. As they go through the door, the band music peaks and finishes)

(Dr. Dempster appears at the desk stage right, in her white coat, facing Delia, who is wearing a street coat over her tap outfit)

Dempster Is it your father's pills?

Delia I think it's meant to be me as well.

Dempster Why, what ails you?

Delia He wants you to check up on me.

Dempster You shouldn't be walking the streets like that, you'll catch your death.

Delia There's a lot of it about.

Dempster Don't you smart-talk me, madam.

(Pause)

Delia He's frightened that I'm going to turn out like my mother.

Dempster He needn't be.

Delia Was she clinically insane, do you think?

Dempster We're not discussing your mother.

Delia You wouldn't happen to know where she is?

Dempster That's quite enough! *(Pause)* You're entitled to grieve for what has happened. But grief is no licence for cheek and misconduct.

Delia Yes, doctor.

Dempster Your mother came of fine stock. Four generations of bishops and high-court judges, that's how strong her mind was. . .

Delia Why the past tense?

Dempster . . . but she was also possessed of a delicacy of feeling. I'm saying no more, run on home now.

Delia She'll never be dead as long as I draw breath.

Dempster Don't flatter yourself, madam. There wasn't a trace of show-off in her, nor self-centredness either. You're a Quinn. Through and through.

(Pause)

Delia Is that what you want me to tell him?

Dempster You can tell him I'm a medical doctor and I can't prescribe a cure for a spoilt child.

Delia It's an odd phrase, that. Like failed priest. Or fallen woman.

Dempster His pills are with the receptionist.

Delia I hope your own father is keeping better.

Dempster Not particularly, thank you.

Delia Just think, Dr. Dempster – you hands were the first that were ever laid on me.

Dempster On you and scores of others, young lady.

Delia Oh, I know. It was nothing personal.

(Delia exits. Dempster frowns, then follows)
(Muzak starts. Quinn appears upstage left, holding aloft a remote-control switch. Vance is at his shoulder)
(Quinn presses the switch and the muzak stops abruptly)

Quinn — **Eh?**
(He starts the muzak again, smiles at Vance, then stops it again)
All right?

Vance — **Throughout the premises?**

Quinn — **Two separate circuits. Organ hymns for the Selection and Reposing Rooms. This one everywhere else.**

Vance — **I congratulate you, Mr Quinn.**

Quinn — **Tasteful, you see. Dignified. But nothing mournful about it.**

Vance — **Yes.**

Quinn — **Mournfulness is the first thing to avoid, Mervyn. Now, that suit, for example.**

Vance — **Too dark?**

Quinn — **In actual fact, it appears black.**

Vance — **There is a grey line. . .**

Quinn — **I see it indeed, and it's a nice-enough looking suit, but you take the point. Apperances. Clients don't want reminded. Black ties, armbands, doleful faces – no, not nowadays, the client wants normality. Mind you, I'm not saying you turn up on the doorstep in a loud check singing Yankee Doodle Dandy.**

Vance — **I understand.**

Quinn — **But you're not a glorified gravedigger either. You're a respected family adviser, along with the doctor and the solicitor. A professional man. So you dress and act accordingly.**

Vance — **Point taken.**
(Quinn leads the way to the desk stage left)

Quinn — **Now then. You're on your way to a First Call. What are you taking along with you?**

Vance — **The arrangements briefcase.**

Quinn — **Containing?**

Vance — **Arrangements forms, list of charges, coffin and casket brochures and photographs.**

Quinn — **Good. So you're in the house. I'm the client. And I'm raving and howling uncontrollably. Heels kicking the settee. Tears tripping me. Over to you.**

Vance — **Please accept. . . our deepest sympathy. For your tragic loss. Rest assured, we will do all in our power to ease the burden. . .**

Quinn — **Hopeless.**

Vance — **Ah.**

Quinn	Weeping and bawling redoubled. You see, Mervyn, it's not just learning our business that counts — but also learning what isn't our business. A crucial distinction. E.g. Efficient disposition of the deceased — our business. The private emotions of the bereaved — no business of ours.
Vance	You ignore them, then?
Quinn	An attitude of polite neutrality. You neither sympathise nor reproach. Like the doctor and the lawyer. Non-judgmental.
Vance	What if the client goes on crying?
Quinn	Describe your demeanour coming into the room.
Vance	Businesslike. . . efficient. . . dignified?
Quinn	Overriding all that. . . you have authority. Relaxed professional authority. To the client, you see, that's bracing. Calming.
Vance	Authority and relaxed.
Quinn	But — let's say the storm still rages on. Now, there's invariably another party in the room, a bit calmer. A neighbour, maybe, or relative. You say to them — I shall wait outside to let Mrs Brown have the chance to compose herself. You convey authority. Along with the sense that you're in no hurry. You are a reassuring figure of professional expertise who is at their disposal. It never fails.
Vance	Of course, yes, it makes sense.
Quinn	You'll find, by the way, that type of client will tend to be down the ladder a bit, educationally speaking.
Vance	The emotional kind?
Quinn	The higher the educational level, the more composed the client.
Vance	Stands to reason.
Quinn	The lower the noisier. As a matter of fact, that had a lot to do with your getting this job, Mervyn.
Vance	How do you mean?
Quinn	Your degree. When you take over the new branch, you'll be servicing a different sort of parish than down here.
Vance	Suburbia.
Quinn	New estates. Skilled workers, in the main. It's a maxim in the business — the funeral director should always be just one degree higher than his parish. Otherwise no authority. You'll get on very well up there.
Vance	With the benefit of your experience, Mr. Quinn.
Quinn	We all share a big responsibility, Mervyn. To the profession. That comes first.
Vance	Quite.
Quinn	You see, we haven't always enjoyed the high standing in society that is ours today. Even in my young days, the so-

called undertaker was socially ostracised by and large. He was an agent of doom. Of course there was a shocking amount of charlatanism and amateurishness in those days.

Vance From a strictly business point of view — the profession seems to me to be almost in its infancy.

Quinn That's the God's own truth, Mervyn. And it has everything to do with the excitement of the job. We're in the pioneering phase. But. . . it's fatally easy to get carried away. You must never forget — you're first and foremost a professional adviser. And only secondarily a salesman.

Vance Sales are what make profits, of course.

Quinn Take it from me, there's only one way to make a worthwhile profit. Give the customer what he wants. And charge him only for what he gets. I can't abide crookedness in any shape or form, Mervyn. You wouldn't believe the rackets some people get up to in this business. It harms the profession's image, but there's more than that to consider. There's the man upstairs. *(He gestures to heaven)* He's the sleeping partner in this enterprise. I firmly believe in keeping on the right side of him, Mervyn.

Vance Absolutely.

Quinn It might be out of fashion in some quarters, but not round this way. *(Pause)* Where were we?

Vance You were mentioning Sales.

Quinn So I was. The point being, our main product is service. That's what we're selling to the public first and foremost, not the hardware. We're not just glorified reps for the florist and the coffin factory.

Vance Though I'd be interested to hear about the arrangements that you have with them.

Quinn We'll get to the small print in due course, Mervyn.

Vance Sorry.

Quinn I just want to impress on you the values in this profession. As I see them. You'll have noticed this.

(He indicates an embroidered text in a frame on the desk)

Vance *(reading)* 'And the light shineth in darkness; and the darkness comprehended it not'. Beautifully worked.

Quinn My wife was a fine needle-woman. In her young days.

Vance Mrs. Quinn? She did this?

Quinn The firm's motto, Vance. We're bringing light into the gloom of superstition and fear. We're letting in warm sunshine to the dark corners. That's the service we offer the client, and believe you me, he deeply appreciates it. We get thank-you letters by the lorry-load. So much for the critics.

Vance Critics?

Quinn Oh, there's always people ready to criticise in any walk of life. The smart set. The same sort that's richly amused by our calling. The sort that has a good old snigger every time it's mentioned.

Vance Up until the moment when they find they have a corpse in the lounge.

Quinn Crudely put, Mervyn, but the point is sound enough. Anyway. That's enough nattering for the moment. I want you to read through these – invoices for the past few months. And this is the Diary. All the details of every funeral we handle are entered here, as they arrive – like a log-book. That'll fill you in on the pattern of business we handle.

Vance Splendid.

Quinn And by the way – don't hesitate, if you see room for improvement anywhere. Speak your piece. It's liberty hall round this way.

Vance Thanks

(He gets involved in the invoices. Quinn begins to work at the desk also)

(Albert Bell has meanwhile come in through the outer door and passed on through to the public room, where he sets up two trestles. On his way back out he encounters Delia arriving, in her school uniform, carrying a large Bible)

Delia Hello, Albert.

Bell Is it young Delia or what?

Delia The very self-same.

Bell I hardly know you this weather, you're growing up too fast.

Delia Are you still at the wrestling game, Albert?

Bell Ah, just the odd bout, to show the young fellows how it's done *(Indicating her Bible)* What's this here, are you turning into a Bible scholar now?

Delia *(handing it to him)* It's for a school project. Though I recommend it if you're looking for a good read.

Bell *(looking through it)* Pictures and all.

Delia There's even a bit of wrestling for you, Jacob versus the Angel. Speaking of which, is Quinn around?

Bell So fas as I know, Delia.

Delia Would you tell him from me that Miss Gault is on her way to see him. . .

Bell Oh lord, are you in her bad books again?

Delia I don't know but I'm trying to avoid her. . . *(the door opens)* . . . oh shit, too late. . . *(but it's Vincent Kane who enters)*

Kane This body out here is growing a beard.

Bell Don't fret, I'm coming.

Kane Hiya, Delia.

Delia Hello, Mr. Kane.

Kane That was a great number you did at the firm's do.

Delia Thank you.

Kane You know, you and me should team up, I've won prizes for my *paso doble.*

(He suddenly sweeps her round the floor in a comic Latin embrace)

Bell It's a credit to you, with feet like them.

Kane Light, bright and nimble, old hand.

Delia *(giggling)* Listen, I've got to get out of here. . .

Bell Don't embarass the child.

Kane This is no child, this is a star of the dance!

(Vance appears. Awkward silence)

Delia Oh, well. Midnight strikes again. *(She takes the Bible from Bell)* My pumpkin awaits. *(She exits)*

Vance Sorry, I was just wondering about the Mulligan remains – have they been collected yet?

Bell We're taking them through now to the Embalming Room, boss.

Vance I thought I'd just keep the Diary straight.

Kane Yes, you do that, Mr. Vance.

(He and Bell start out, but as they reach the door, Miss Gault appears in it. She is brought face to face with Vance as she enters. Kane and Bell go on out)

Gault Vance!

Vance Hello, Miss Gault.

Gault What on earth are you doing here? I hope that nobody . . . . I mean, you haven't lost anyone, I hope.

Vance No, I work for the firm.

Gault For Quinn's?

Vance Mr. Quinn has engaged me as his personal assistant.

(Kane and Bell re-enter, carrying a 'shell' or temporary coffin. They pass by Gault and Vance en route to the public room)

While I get to know the business.

Gault Physics was your subject, as I recall.

Vance *(Deadpan)* The law of falling bodies. *(Kane and Bell plant the 'shell' on the trestles, and depart)* I switched to Business Studies.

Gault How do you like it?

Vance It's a good firm. There's a branch opening in the New Year which I'm to take over. It's a business with a lot of growth potential.

Gault *(Deadpan)* For the daisies, certainly.

(Pause)

Vance I trust you haven't suffered a bereavement yourself, Miss Gault?

Gault No, no, just visiting, thank God. I was hoping to have a word with Mr. Quinn.

Vance Certainly. You'll find him in the office there.

Gault Good. Well. Nice to see our former pupils prosper.

Vance You're looking very well yourself, Miss Gault.

Gault Am I?

Vance I see you've let your hair grow.

Gault You've had yours cut, Vance.

Vance Mr. Quinn recommended it.

Gault Good for him. Well, very best wishes in your new employ.

Vance I'd like to drop in at school some day.

Gault Do. *(He exits. She proceeds down to Quinn's desk)*

Quinn Miss Gault! *(With a flourish, he reveals a deck of cards spread in his right hand)* Come in. Take a seat. Pick a card.

Gault Any card?

Quinn That's the style.

Gault *(As she takes a card and sits)* You seem full of beans, Mr. Quinn.

Quinn Speaking of which – coffee?

Gault Thank you, no.

Quinn A glass of sherry, perhaps?

Gault Well – maybe I'll have a coffee after all.

(Quinn presses the buzzer on his office intercom)

Quinn Back in the deck. I'm not looking.

Girl Employee *(On intercom)* Yes, sir?

Quinn *(To intercom as Gault replaces the card)* Gillian, will you bring in one coffee, please, and will you refer all calls to Mr. Vance. *(As he shuffles the deck)* Tell me one thing, Miss Gault – how do you manage to look years younger every time I see you?

Gault You're the magician, not me.

Quinn *(Giving her the deck)* Find your card. That's a most handsome dress, if I may say so.

Gault Thank you. *(After giving the cards a perfunctory riffle)* It's not here.

Quinn How very mysterious, are you sure? The Lost Card, eh?

Gault I've come to talk about Delia, Mr. Quinn.

(The Girl Employee enters with a coffee tray which she places on the desk)

Quinn Thank you, Gillian. Hang on, what's that stuck behind your ear there? *(He plucks a card from her head. She proceeds on out without any particular reaction, being used to this)*

My goodness, the Queen of Hearts.

Gault — Very impressive. She's become a serious problem.

Quinn — Ah.

Gault — Her behaviour has grown increasingly wayward. To the point where she's seriously disrupting the work of her whole class.

Quinn — Up to her tricks again?

Gault — That certainly seems an apt way of putting it. If she were in a lower form, I'd be asking you to remove her from the shool. Since she has less than a year to go, I'm reluctant to do that. However, her behaviour is quite intolerable and will have to change.

Quinn — A rueful plight, Miss Gault, to be handicapped by your own special gifts.

Gault — The girls from the upper school went on a museum visit last Thursday. They're doing a study project on Ancient Egypt.

Quinn — Aha. That'll be why she was quizzing me about mummification.

Gault — Doubtless. On account of Delia's behaviour, they were asked to leave the museum.

Quinn — Horseplay.

Gault — Amongst other things, she threw herself across one of the exhibits shouting, 'Mummy, mummy, it's you, it's you!' *(Pause)* It's not funny when you have to repair the damage of such behaviour. Which I think you'll agree qualifies as hooliganism rather than precocity.

Quinn — So far as any damage done – I'll have a cheque made out at once.

Gault — That won't be necessary. However . . . .

Quinn — Words will be spoken.

Gault — She herself doesn't suffer, you see. The gifted ones don't. It's the dimwits who are influenced by her. They can't afford to slack.

Quinn — I did send her to see Dr. Dempster, as a matter of fact.

Gault — Not a psychiatrist by any chance?

Quinn — Oh, no, no. Just our G.P. The family doctor. A fine sensible woman. I knew she'd be able to offer a good private heart-to heart natter. Delia misses her mother, you know.

Gault — May I ask if there is any news of Mrs. Quinn?

Quinn — Not a whisper, I'm afraid. For over a year.

Gault — The police have found no trace of her?

Quinn — Oh, the police drop their enquiries on a missing person after six months. How's your coffee?

Gault — Finished, thank you.

Quinn Let me get rid of that cup for you.
(He picks up the tray, then removes the empty cup, sets it on the desk in front of him, and drapes the napkin over it)

Gault Forgive me for asking this, but how exactly did it happen?

Quinn One windy day — the sun shining out of a clear blue sky — she went down to the florist's.

Gault And?

Quinn That's all. *(He taps the napkin-covered cup twice on the desk. Then instead of a third tap, he smashes the napkin down flat. It is as if the cup had gone through the desk)*

Gault *(Trying her best to ignore this)* You mean she just vanished?
(Quinn brings the unbroken cup out from under the desk and sets it back in its saucer)

Quinn She was mad about flowers, Agnes. A passionate gardener. Though she really loved wild flowers best, oddly enough. But she was a great help to me. Particularly with the florist's orders. Sprays, wreaths, crosses, chaplets etc. I was only a few months in business, on my own account. Before that I was a Branch Manager with Fullerton's. She went out this day with several orders, just as usual. She never arrived at the florist's. And she never came home again.

Gault You don't have any . . . any idea . . .?

Quinn Amnesia. Most likely. She could be anywhere. A different name . . . sleepwalking, in a way. Some day, some little thing, could jolt her wide awake. Who knows?
(Pause)

Gault I suppose we're all like that, one way or another.

Quinn Beg pardon?

Gault I'm sorry, I was . . . I mean, it must be terrible for you. A nightmare.

Quinn No, no, nothing of the sort. You learn acceptance in this job, Miss Gault. There's no room for melancholy in our trade. It's a real vocation, you know. In fact, it's a way of life.

Gault I've never thought of it quite like that.

Quinn So long as you're here, let me show you round the premises.

Gault Well, I'm afraid I really don't have the time just now . . .

Quinn Miss Gault — surely not squeamishness from a lady of your sophistication?

Gault Somehow my thirst for knowledge just stops short of funeral parlours.

Quinn No shock-horror round this way. Nothing macabre. Nothing up our sleeves. Just dealing in a decent businesslike manner with an everyday law of nature.

Gault Perhaps another time.

Quinn Promise?

Gault Yes. All right. *(She rises)*

Quinn Another time, then. *(He escorts her to the door)* And I hope you'll come through to the house for dinner after. I'll ring you later in the week to arrange a day, will that suit?

Gault That's fine.

Quinn Very good. *(They exit together)*

(Delia is discovered in the armchair stage right, with the Bible open on her lap)

Delia The smooth man. That was Jacob. Esau was the hairy one. 'Behold Esau my brother is a hairy man, and I am a smooth man.' *(She starts looking through the Bible)*

(The Dean is discovered, upstage right, standing holding a scrap of paper, in a public-speaking posture)

Dean You know, this occasion puts me in mind of the first funeral I ever officiated at. *(To himself)* No, perhaps I'd better rephrase that. *(Public again)* At any rate, I well recall the days when the coffin would always be carried all the way to the graveside. There might just be one hired limousine to take the older folk, with everyone else on foot. So there I was, with a chronic bunion, hobbling along, still a good mile from the cemetery gates. And greatly relieved when the undertaker said to me, Excuse me, Reverend, but would you like a lift? Having graciously accepted this kind offer, the next thing I know is, I've become one of the pallbearers. What he meant by a lift, you see, was a lift of the coffin. *(Pause. To himself)* Sounds laboured . . . a lighter touch . . . *(Public again)* You know, this function takes me back to the days of what I believe you in the trade call a walking funeral . . . *(To himself)* No, that'll never do. *(He gets engrossed in rewriting)*

(Light full on Delia again)

Delia *(Reading)* And Jacob was left alone. And there wrestled a man with him until the breaking of the day.

(Gong. The curtain rises on the inner stage, revealing a little wrestling ring. Vincent Kane, in wrestling shorts and boots, is asleep in a corner. Into the opposite corner climbs Albert Bell, also in wrestling gear, but with the added features of a silver hood and tiny angel's wings. Delia's back is to them throughout the scene, which is of course occurring in her imagination)

Kane *(Springing up)* God Almighty!

Delia That's one interpretation.

(Bell wrestles Kane into an arm lock)

Kane	Who is this? Why does he want me to wrestle? I'm no wrestler.
Delia	I wouldn't exactly say that. Look at this – 'He took his brother by the heel in the womb' – and that was only the start of it.
	(Kane suddenly slips free. He and Bell circle)
Delia	A smooth man.
Bell	A slippery-looking customer.
Kane	So that's who he is – Esau, the brother?
Delia	That's another interpretation.
	(Kane lunges, Bell falls, but manages a deft scissors which pins Kane to the floor)
Delia	There was the business of his birthright too.
Kane	He made me an offer.
Delia	You robbed him blind.
Kane	A mess of pottage.
Delia	Some bargain.
Kane	Fair and square. I gave him my lentils.
Delia	Just what is pottage, anyway?
	(Kane pushes Bell in the face and gets free. They circle)
Delia	Then you swindled him out of the father's blessing.
Kane	The mother put me up to that.
Delia	Dressing up in goatskins to make yourself hairy.
	(Bell gets a hold on Kane, picks him up and holds him above his head)
	And when Esau heard the words of his father, he cried with a great and exceeding bitter cry, and said unto his father, Bless me, even me also, O my father.
	(Bell throws Kane to the ground)
Kane	Leave me in peace!
Delia	After that you ran away to your uncle's house and got rich.
	(Kane gets up, staring at Bell)
	Now it's fourteen years later and you're travelling back home. Tomorrow morning you have to face your brother Esau again. Tonight you're on your own. And it's yourself you have to wrestle with.
	(Kane grabs Bell and holds him in a neck lock)
Delia	That's my interpretation, for what it's worth.
Kane	I will not let thee go, except thou bless me!
Delia	You're a terrible man for the blessings.
Kane	Tell me, I pray thee, thy name!
Delia	And when he saw that he prevailed not against him, he touched the hollow of his thigh; and the hollow of Jacob's thigh was out of joint, as he wrestled with him.

(Bell wrenches free and claws a hand down Kane's thigh, leaving a red track. Kane howls with pain. The inner stage is flooded in red. Bell lifts Kane up, kisses his head, lifts his arm in victory to the sound of triumphant music. Kane embraces him as the curtain falls on the inner stage, as the light goes out on Delia, and as that on the Dean comes up again. He is now holding a drink)

Dean — **The mystery to me is – why was it not contested? Now that's the bit I don't understand, John. Why did Dr. Dempster not contest it, do you think?**

(Quinn is discovered upstage of the Dean, unpacking a parcel)

Quinn — **Maybe the fight's gone out of her, Dean – now that old boy Dempster's finally passed on.**

Dean — **It's a matter of what was rightfully hers, though.**

Quinn — **Maybe the peace and quiet is enough to do her, they were at each other's throats right up to the last.**

Dean — **Twenty-seven years she nursed the old boy and I doubt if ever a soft word passed between them. He used to brag that he'd outlive her, you know.**

Quinn — **Damned near did, too. He was a stubborn old cuss all right.**

Dean — **And at the end of the road, sweet fanny adam. He leaves every penny to the younger one in New Zealand, that ran away as a schoolgirl.**

Quinn — **The doctor got the practice.**

Dean — **Didn't she work her passage to get it, for half a lifetime?**

Quinn — **By the way, Dean, how's the new verger doing?**

Dean — **Very little life about him, John.**

Quinn — **The old fellow was great value.**

Dean — **A heart of corn, and a man could do the needful without always needing it pointed out to him.**

Quinn — **But not the new chap.**

Dean — **The labourer is worth his hire, John. What can you expect? If you don't pay the rate for the job?**

Quinn — **This is the modern world.**

Dean — **The going rate, I don't care if it's serving lunches or serving summonses or serving the Lord. A fair day's pay is called for, and the church is not providing it.**

Quinn — **Result – a drop in standards.**

Dean — **Low recruitment. Mediocre material. You have to pay the rate for the job if you've got the slightest hope of growth. Otherwise goodnight.**

(Quinn has now unpacked the parcel: it contains a strait-jacket. He goes to the door)

Quinn — *(Calling)* **Delia!**

Dean What about this new assistant of yours?

Quinn Mervyn Vance? Only first-class, Dean. A natural-born funeral director if ever I spotted one. He'll go places, I've no doubt about that. *(Calls)* Delia!

Dean The incentive's there, you see, John . . .

Quinn Where has that girl got to?

Dean It makes all the difference.

Quinn Pardon me for a moment, Dean. *(He exits)*

(The Dean scrutinises his scrap of paper again)

Dean *(After reflecting for a moment)* So the good man's brother comes up to me and says, you'll maybe be wanting a lift, Reverend? Little realising just what he meant, I of course replied . . .

Delia *(Entering)* Thy name shall be called no more Jacob but Israel.

Dean What's that?

Delia Nuncle.

Dean Well well well, and how's that favourite niece of mine, eh?

Delia Who do you think was Jacob's opponent in the wrestling match?

Dean Jacob? Jacob and the angel is it you mean?

Delia In Genesis he's described just as a man.

Dean Is that so? For your school homework, is it?

Delia I think the angel comes from a later reference in Hosea, 'Yea, he had power over the angel and prevailed'. On the other hand, both of them actually suggest that it could be God himself, 'I have seen God face to face and my life is preserved'.

Dean Of course those old stories are a bit of a mish-mash, you know.

Delia That one's the best in the book, I think. A wrestling match with the God inside.

Dean You've certainly been reading it up anyway.

Delia I'm working my way from cover to cover.

Dean Good for you, child. You'll be wanting to concentrate on the Gospels, of course.

Delia No, I prefer the Old Testament. It seems more true to life.

Quinn *(Re-entering)* Talk about a vanishing act — I've been searching high and low and you're here all along.

Dean Something of a Bible scholar to boot, John.

Quinn Here, look at this that I got today.

Dean Chapter and verse off pat.

(Delia examines the straitjacket)

Delia What's the trick?

Quinn It's an old escape dodge. See these loops? You keep hold of them while the jacket's being laced up. Then you let go the

	slack – and goodnight Harry Houdini. Want to try it?
Delia	**Why not?**
Quinn	**Watch this now, Dean.** *(He puts the straitjacket on Delia)*
Delia	**The thing is, Dean – was it the Father or the Holy Ghost? . . .**
Dean	**What's that?**
Delia	**. . . who was the wrestler in the family?**
Dean	**Oh, I see! Well now, what you have to remember is, those were the primitive days, Delia. Ancient Tales of the Patriarchs. A ragged band of desert nomads. Simple folk. The understanding of God being very elementary.**
Delia	**A personal God.**
Dean	**Absolutely.**
Delia	**A God you could get your mitts on. Feel him squirming in your gut. Face up to him in your own reflection.**
Dean	**Then again, a lot of those old yarns were just made up to explain the meaning of a well-known place-name.**
Delia	**Penuel.**
Dean	**What's that?**
Delia	**The place they wrestled at was Penuel.**
Dean	**There you are.**
Quinn	**There you go. Try that.**
Delia	**Face of God, it means.** *(She starts to wriggle)* **I have seen God face to face. Wrestled him to the ground. First he cripples you. Then he gives you his blessing.** *(She goes into a fury of writhing and twisting. Finally she wrenches the straitjacket off, flings it to the ground and begins to cry bitterly)*
Quinn	**Dilly dearest, it's all right, don't be frightened . . .** *(She stops crying as suddenly as she started, and picks up the straightjacket)*
Delia	**I just wondered if my mother might be in need of one like this.** *(She hands the straightjacket to the Dean and goes to the armchair stage left, where she curls up. Pause)*
Dean	**Highly strung, John . . .** *(Embarrassed even more by the unwitting pun)* **I mean, a sensitive nature.**
Quinn	**Just a slight panic. I'll go and talk a while to her.**
Dean	**I'll toddle on, then.**
Quinn	**Wait, though . . . there was something you came round to discuss.**
Dean	**It was only the talk.**
Quinn	**The talk?**
Dean	**The talk for the Association of Funeral Directors.**
Quinn	**Oh, there's just a few words called for. Along with the prayer.**
Dean	**It's a question of hitting the right note, though.**
Quinn	**No problem, Dean.**

Dean I'll stop by tomorrow again.

Quinn Do indeed. Goodnight now.

(The Dean exits. Quinn crosses to where Delia crouches in the chair)

Quinn Dilly, love? Is the old man forgiven?

(Pause)

Delia You never sing that anymore.

Quinn What, 'Dilly Dilly'?

Delia Used to work wonders on the childish grief.

Quinn *(Singing)* Lavender green, dilly, dilly,
Lavender green,
I'll be your king, dilly dilly,
You'll be my queen . . .

Delia You're a bit rusty on the lyrics.

Quinn And after that you'd always demand a story.

Delia You'd a terrible memory for those as well.

Quinn Fairy tales, Bible stories. Anything.

(Pause)

Delia Tell me the Sleeping Beauty.

Quinn What, now?

Delia Don't panic. I'll keep you straight.

Quinn The Sleeping Beauty . . . right. Let's see. Once upon a time.

Delia So far so good.

Quinn There was a king and queen. To whom was born. A little princess. And . . .they invited to her christening party . . . some of the fairy folk.

Delia Seven. Seven fairies.

Quinn Seven fairies, who all brought her gifts. Of various kinds.

Delia Beauty. Wit. Grace. Playing, Dancing and Singing.

Quinn That's only six.

Delia The seventh was held in reserve. The seventh would be the kiss. But the curse had to happen first.

Quinn The curse, that's right. From some bad old fairy they'd all forgotten about, who lit on the king and queen and declared, as soon as this child pricks her thumb on a spindle, she shall die. And then the seventh spoke up and said, this curse I cannot cancel. But my gift is – the princess will not die – but only sleep.

Delia For a hundred years.

Quinn For a hundred years, and then a prince will come along. And waken her with a kiss. So the princess grew up, until she was a lovely girl of sixteen.

Delia The king having banned spindles from the palace. But sure what use was that. The wound has to happen first. There always has to be the wound. Before there can be the kiss.

Quinn So one day the princess found this room in the attic, and there was an old lady spinning. This old lady hadn't heard about the king's command. The princess asked to try her hand at the wheel . . . and rightaway pricked her thumb . . .

Delia First he cripples you. And then he gives you his blessing. If you're lucky.

Quinn Eh?

Delia Tell me the rest.

Quinn So the princess fell into a deep sleep. Well – a hundred years passed by.

Delia Don't forget the forest.

Quinn Was there a forest?

Delia The fairy caused a forest to grow around the castle, to protect the princess as she lay asleep. When the prince finally appeared, hunting, the trees leaned back to let him through, closing behind him again. He didn't know what lay ahead – but he couldn't go back either. He must have wondered what in the name of God was going on.

Quinn At last he came to the door of the castle and pushed it open on its rusty hinges.

Delia She couldn't stand the smell, Quinn.

Quinn Was there a smell?

Delia The smell of white lilies and dark heavy clothes. Polished wood and sanctity and guilt and grief, the smog of the funeral industry.

Quinn You know, we should be rehearsing for the Association's do . . .

Delia She couldn't bear it and she ran away.

Quinn No . . .

Delia She might have taken me with her at least.

Quinn Don't be hard on the old man, Dilly.

Delia Talk to me about it!
(Pause)

Quinn Too much imagination, you see. The work put a strain on her, there's no doubt. She'd no professional objectivity. She suffered alongside every client. You can't afford to do that, any more than a doctor or a nurse. A load on your mind like that . . . she didn't want to abandon us. She loved us.

Delia A hundred years is a long time.

Quinn Don't you fret. It'll be all right.
(Pause)
Hey. *(He stands up)* Come on and we'll fit up the box, eh? For the skeleton joke – eh? Eh?

(She wearily follows him out. Bell and Kane enter, carrying a coffin, which they set beside the one already in the public room. Vance is escorting them)

Vance — No, I'm afraid he left a message that he wouldn't be in at all.

Kane — He was meant to be meeting a delegation this afternoon, it was arranged a week ago.

Vance — Well, if it's anything I can deal with, Vincent . . .

Kane — It's union business, Mr. Vance.

Vance — Which reminds me. *(He takes an envelope from his pocket and hands it to Kane)* My membership application.

Kane — You're joining?

Vance — Oh, yes.

Kane — You realise Mr. Quinn won't have any truck with the union?

Vance — Really? We've never discussed it. Oh, excuse me, lads . . . *(Dempster has entered)* Good afternoon, can I be of service?

Dempster — Yes, you can go and tell Quinn that Dr. Dempster wants to see him.

Vance — I'm sorry, Doctor, but Mr. Quinn is out of the office today. Perhaps I can be of help?
(Bell and Kane quietly slip out during this)

Dempster — Who are you?

Vance — I'm Mervyn Vance, his assistant manager. If it's in connection with the interment of your father, Doctor, I assisted Mr. Quinn in all the arrangements . . .

Dempster — You don't look old enough for this work.

Vance — I'm doing my best to learn.

Dempster — Except for your eyes, they're old enough. They look as if they're peering out of a crypt. I'm here to order another funeral, as it happens.
(Bell and Kane re-enter, carrying another coffin: they place it alongside the other two during the following, and exit)

Vance — Certainly, Doctor. If you care to come this way, I'll be glad to make a note of the particulars. *(He leads her to the desk, holds the chair for her to be seated, and sits down himself)* Now then.

Dempster — The particulars are few. The funeral in question is my own.
(Pause)

Vance — Yes. *(He opens a drawer and takes out a form)*

Dempster — What's that?

Vance — Just a standard form, Doctor.

Dempster — What kind of form?

Vance — Well – it's what we call an N.Y.D. Form.

Dempster Meaning?

Vance Not Yet Deceased.

(Pause)

Dempster You know, Death has been personified in many different ways throughout history, Vance. I might have know that today's version would be a cryptic little bureaucrat.

Vance The form is only a convenience for us, Doctor. Just to ensure that everything's cut and dried.

Dempster A singularly unhappy turn of phrase.

Vance If you'd sooner dispense with it . . .

Dempster Let's just allow the N.Y.D. to rest in peace, shall we.

(Vance puts the form away)

I'm here because I'll be dead within a few months, and I wish to be disposed of in my own way. Not in Quinn's way or anybody else's. If there were some form of Do-It-Yourself funeral, that's what I'd choose. I could always jump into the sea, of course, but it's not really my style unfortunately. Temperamentally I seem to be drawn to the slower and messier forms of suicide. Like thirty-five years of solitary drinking, say. Though it wasn't all suicide in my case, actually There was also an element of murder involved.

(Pause)

Vance A cup of coffee, Doctor?

Dempster Quinn's wife used to be his assistant, you know.

Vance Yes.

Dempster Speaking of murder.

Vance I gather she was of a rather nervous disposition.

Dempster She lacked your equanimity.

Vance I'm trying to learn the methodical and professional way to do the job.

Dempster You certainly have a prize teacher. And I expect my precise instructions to be conveyed to him, is that understood?

Vance Of course.

Dempster I'm presenting various organs to medical science. If nothing else, my liver will serve as an awful warning to drunken students. However, I want the rest interred in my family's plot in the cemetery. Buried on symbolic grounds, you might say. The Last of the Dempsters. So – you will collect my carcass from the hospital, deposit it in a plain wooden box without ornamentation of any kind, conduct it to the cemetery and bury it. There are to be no religious rites, no other people present, either here or at the graveside, no processions, obsequies, or hypocrisies of any sort. Is that all quite clear?

Vance Perfectly.

Dempster My solicitor will pay the bill. Cash on delivery.

Vance Very well.

(Bell and Kane have entered with another coffin, which they place beside the other three)

Dempster *(Rising)* So that's that. Good-bye, Vance.

Vance Good-bye, Doctor, and thank you. *(He walks towards the door with her)*

Dempster I don't expect to be seeing you again. Though you, of course, will have the pleasure of seeing me.

(The Dean enters through the outer door)

Dean Well, Doctor, is it your good self?

Dempster I'm glad to see you, Dean, I have something for you.

Dean Did I hear right that you're giving up the practice?

Dempster I suppose that's a way of putting it, what do you say, Vance?

Vance If you'll excuse me, please, I must attend to other business. *(He signals to Kane and Bell, waiting by the coffins in the public room, and they all three exit together)*

Dean I know it's none of my business, Doctor . . .

Dempster . . . but?

Dean Well, I was most distressed about the terms of your father's will. I think you deserved better from him.

Dempster Why?

Dean It's a matter of what was rightfully yours. You wouldn't think of contesting it?

(Dempster has been fishing in her handbag)

Dempster Ah, here we are. *(She produces an engraved, gold-plated trowel)* It's the ceremonial trowel used at the laying of the cathedral foundation stone. Presented to my great-great uncle as architect. My father was most emphatic that you should have it after his demise.

Dean Well well well, that was thoughtful indeed.

Dempster You can hold it in reserve for the topping-out ceremony. If the building ever gets finished. How long has it been now, ninety-six years?

Dean It's a matter of hard cash, Doctor. The money wasn't all there when they started, and it's not too easily raised nowadays. There again, building costs these days, for that sort of structure . . .

Dempster So you think the family money should have come my way?

Dean Indeed I do.

Dempster What about your own family money?

Dean Beg pardon?

Dempster That you and Agnes loaned to Quinn? To open this death-factory with?

Dean It's been put to good use, Doctor. John has a very fine business brain, as well you know.

Dempster Not to mention a smooth tongue.

Dean Oh, no, it's soundly invested.

Dempster Except that it's tied up in your sister's name, and now she's vanished.

Dean An unforeseen tragedy, Doctor.

Dempster An act of God, I suppose.

Dean Oh John does a grand job, he would always see me right.

Dempster You still have no news of Agnes?

Dean Not a whisper, no.
(Pause)
What brings you here, Doctor?

Dempster He's quite Uriah Heepish, that young man, isn't he?

Dean Young Vance, is it?

Dempster I was giving him instructions for my funeral.

Dean God grant they'll not be needed for a long while yet, Doctor.

Dempster Not too long, I have cirrhosis of the liver, I'm entering a hospice this afternoon. *(As he makes to speak)* Spare me the pieties, Dean. I made it clear to Vance that I want no mumbo-jumbo when they bury me, and I'm making you personally responsible on that score.

Dean You'll be a heavy loss to us, Doctor.

Dempster I won't be the least loss to anyone. My father and I lived like wrestlers, always grappling for the upper hand. Though it was my mother's ghost in me that he was really wrestling with. At any rate it was a stupid waste of two lives. No sooner does he go down at last for the final time, than I'm pulled down directly after him. You could concoct quite a sermon out of that, Dean. I spend my whole life waiting for my father to die. And it's that very life — that life which I spent — that I'm now dying of in my turn. Yes, you could draw all kinds of homilies from that. However, not over my grave-side, if you don't mind. *(She exits. He follows. The muzak starts, very loud. Vance enters, holding aloft the remote-control switch, and abruptly switches it off)*

Vance That system will have to be replaced. It switches on if some-body slams a door.
(Kane and Bell have followed him with another coffin, which they place alongside the ones already there)
Is that the lot?

Bell Just the one more, boss. *(He exits again)*

Vance They're not really up to much, are they?

Kane The public never notices, Mervyn. Nobody wants to be bothered with the dead these days. *(He exits too. Vance inspects the coffin)*

Vance The fact is, they could be made for a third of the cost. And still look twice as good. There's so much pointless workmanship in them. The whole concept needs to be rethought. *(Bell and Kane re-enter with the sixth and final coffin, which they place alongside the others)*

Kane That applies to more than just the coffins.

Vance You know, I'm interested to hear how chaps like you get started in this business.

Bell In my young day you took any job that was going, and thankful to get it, Mr. Vance. Although personally I like the work. You feel you're doing something for people.

Vance That's certainly true.

Bell Actually, I was put in mind the other day of a story my granny told me once. She recalled a man knocking at the door of her cottage when she was a young widow. It was a boiling hot day and he asked for a drink of water. My granny told him to step on in. I can't, he says, my mother's out here. So my granny told him to bring the mother in too. No, he says, I have her in the wheelbarrow, you see — I'm just on my way to the graveyard to bury her. *(He chuckles)* The ma's body, in the wheelbarrow. At least we've progressed a bit since then, eh? Beautiful premises, like this place. We're a bit more civilised about it now.

Kane The only difference now is, you're pushing the barrow for him and getting a pittance in return.

Bell Right enough, the money's not great.

Vance Hence the national pay claim?

Kane If it's rejected this time, the union's ordering a work-to-rule to commence in ten days' time.

Bell We'd prefer to avoid it if we could, Mr. Vance.

Vance Why?

Kane The bodies will pile up in the mortuaries, that's why. There'll be corpses starting to putrefy in people's back bedrooms.

Bell We don't want to cause distress to the public.

Vance Why not?

Kane Eh?

Vance Surely it's the public who are at fault by your own account.

Bell I don't quite follow you there, Mr. Vance.

Vance Society would prefer to forget what our work entails, right? The one way to remind society would be to withdraw our labour. Suddenly people would have to push their own barrows. I guarantee you that funeral fees would triple overnight, no problem.

Kane We're not after that. The managements are making fat profits as things are, they can afford to meet our claim.

Vance You'd be surprised. And anyway, within a year, the issue will arise again, and again and again after that. No, best to call an all-out strike and have done with it, I'd say. A bout of quick drastic surgery is better than years of ineffective medicine.

(Pause)

Kane I take your point all right.

Vance Good. It seems to me a business that needs a bit of a shaking-up.

Bell Vince – we ought to collect that order from the printer's.

Kane Sure.

Vance I'll come with you, I want to ask that printer a few questions.

(They exit. Quinn and Miss Gault appear from stage right, holding large glasses of sherry. Miss Gault is laughing)

Quinn Share the gag, come on.

Gault *(Surpressing her laughter)* No, really, it's just a very silly thought. *(They pass on into the public room and she sees the line of six coffins)* Aha. Death Row.

Quinn This is our Selection Room.

(Gault bursts out laughing again)

Gault I'm sorry, I'm sorry – this is awful – but I keep on thinking it's all like a high-class whorehouse.

Quinn *(Mock shock)* Miss Gault!

Gault I know, I'm sorry, but it's all the carpeting and the chandeliers and all those names – interview rooms and preparation rooms, not to mention the reposing rooms. *(They both laugh. Pause)*

Quinn I love that laugh of yours, you know.

Gault You what?

Quinn The way you laugh with your whole body.

Gault I don't suppose there's much of that goes on around here.

Quinn Not amongst the clients, no. The rest of us stay cheerful, though.

Gault You're certainly full enough of life. How can you go on like that surrounded by all of this?

Quinn You could ask the same of a surgeon.

Gault Only a very incompetent surgeon.

Quinn The fact is, this work enhances life. It makes you more aware than most of your blessed five senses. It sharpens your hunger for life. *(Pause. They are standing quite close together. Gault breaks away)*

Gault And this is the firm's showroom? I suppose these are the latest models?

Quinn Just our standard coffin types. These are the elms – Park, Consul, Ascot – and these ones are the oaks – Crown, Royal, and Doric.

Gault Good God, they sound like brands of cigarettes.

Quinn What could be more appropriate?

Gault Spoken like a non-smoker.

Quinn Apropos of which, we have a range of cremation urns as well.

Gault But why would anyone want to choose a coffin? What does it matter?

Quinn Your final resting-place. It may as well be a decent one.

Gault But it's only your old cadaver.

Quinn Think of how much you owe it.

Gault It's curious, but I've never really thought about my own death. I mean the actual physical event as opposed to the abstract idea.

Quinn All the music you've heard. And the birdsong and the sea. The food you've eaten and the Spring sun on your face . . . the smell of the ground. Your body gave you the world. The least you can give it back is a nice box. *(Pause)*

Gault What an extraordinary man you are. *(He kisses her. She responds, then moves away)* We'd better go.

Quinn You're magnificent.

Gault Please . . .

Quinn A vibrant strong lovely woman.

Gault Don't be so foolish.

Quinn A miracle, Miss Gault. You can't stop me feeling that. *(They kiss again. She is more responsive, but breaks off again)*

Gault This is grotesque. This room . . .

Quinn We'll go through to the house.

Gault I really don't think we should.

Quinn You promised.

Gault Apart from anything else, you're a married man.

Quinn No.

Gault Well, your wife may have disappeared, but you're still . . .

Quinn I'm not married.

Gault What do you mean?

Quinn I'm a widower. *(Pause)* Agnes passed away six months ago. *(Pause)*

Gault How do you know?

Quinn The police. In North London, it was. Traffic accident. She'd been working as a hospital cleaner. No identification. All they found in her handbag were the orders for the florist, with my name on them.

Gault How desperately sad. I'm truly sorry.

Quinn Life was a torment to her. In many ways it was a merciful release.

Gault Why didn't you tell me before?

Quinn Only her brother and I know. The Dean, that is. We arranged for a private cremation. I wanted to keep it from Delia.

Gault But she'll have to be told.

Quinn No. Not yet. She's too vulnerable. When she's older. Stronger. I'll break it to her gradually.

Gault So you've borne it all alone for six months?

Quinn I've got professional status in these matters, don't forget. *(Pause)*

Gault Shall we go through to the house now?
(He nods. She goes to him. As they kiss, the lid of the coffin nearest them is flung back and Delia sits up)

Delia OVER MY DEAD BODY, SUNSHINE!
(Gault backs off, hands to mouth, gasping, then runs out. Quinn, deathly pale, goes after her. As Delia climbs out of the coffin, Vance runs in from stage left, wearing a long black woollen overcoat)

Vance I heard a disturbance, what happened?

Delia Oh, nothing serious – my father was just groping my headmistress, and I was watching from a coffin.

Vance Where's Mr. Quinn?

Delia I think he's chasing her down the street now. Have you ever tried out one of these coffins?

Vance Not in person, no.

Delia You owe it to your clients, Vance. They're very badly insulated. Even Jonah was better off inside his big fish.

Vance Why are you such a frantic little fart?

Delia How'd you like to kiss my arse?

Vance Quite a lot, in fact, from what I've seen of it.

Delia You're a Jonah. You know what that is, don't you? A carrier of evil luck. Like a rat carries plague.

Vance You've heard bad news, is that it?

Delia You've got a Jonah for a soul. Peering out through your fish eyes.

Vance Everyone has it in for my eyes around here.
(She falls to her knees and starts to shiver violently)
What's wrong?

Delia I'm cold. I can't walk.

Vance Here. *(He taks off his coat and wraps it completely round her, raising her to her feet. She starts to faint. He lifts her in his arms. Music starts from off, very loud. The curtain rises on the inner stage. He carries her up on to it. The curtain falls again, the music stops, and Quinn is discovered, downstage right, in evening dress)*

Quinn **Fellow Association members — and ladies — the Dean's tale of getting a 'lift' has put us all in mind I'm sure of similar embarrassing moments. The best laid plans and so on. I know the reddest face I ever had was at an out-of-town affair once. It was a place I'd never been before in my life. The deceased had only recently moved there, you see. Well, I got the cortege off on time . . . but before too long I knew we were hopelessly lost. The street directions made no sense at all. The mourners were all strangers as well. I had to stop the whole cortege and ask some passers-by the way. Nobody seemed to know. We just drove round, hour after hour, more and more desperate, more and more lost . . .** *(He starts to cry. Music from off. He pulls himself together)* **But anyhow, by way of a modest grand finale, my assistant and I have prepared a little surprise. Presto!**

(Gong. Curtain rises on the inner stage, with the box as before and Delia posed beside it in her tap outfit. Quinn joins her, opens the box, pushes it round to show it's empty, tapping on the walls; then he ushers Delia in and closes it. Music continues. He pushes the box round again)

Nothing up our sleeves, folks! No skeletons in our cupboard!

(He opens the box. There's a skeleton inside. He closes it, pretending shock, opens it again, Delia is inside holding a prop dagger. She steps out, sticks it in his heart. He sinks slowly to the ground. She tap-dances downstage. The curtain falls on the inner stage. The music stops. She is in a small pool of light)

Delia **Once upon a time the damsel and the christening. The spell and the spindle and the castle in the forest. Which brings us nearly to the end. What is she, lying there, with her damaged thumb, in a pure dreamless sleep? The prince jangles in, trailing mud, smelling of horse. He has come from a world of furious transactions. His body is all itches and sniffing, ready to kiss. Who is she? A stateless person. An unresolved chord in the waltz of time. He shuffles round the catafalque and peers at her. One kiss would crack this nimbus open, for time to flood her veins again. He bends over the pale, perfect lips, ready to kiss. He looks. He ponders. He hesitates. And, of course, is lost.**

(Blackout. Music: the waltz from Tchaikovky's 'Sleeping Beauty')

ACT TWO

The naked corpse of a young girl (played by the Girl Employee) lies on a bare trolley on the stage left side of the public room, in a pool of light.

Quinn is discovered in the armchair stage right. Beside him is a clothes rack full of elegant dresses. As he talks, he pulls out an impossible number of women's scarves from a top hat on his knee.

Quinn **There's no telling where it might end. Once upon a time it was all winding-sheets and shrouds, nothing but white, now we have the client's own night-wear, at the very least. With a custom-designed dressing gown over that. Pastel shades. Quilted paisley pattern or suchlike. Why not a smart suit? Or a favourite sports outfit? People want to show their best to the world, it's natural. Nature didn't provide too well. A few clumps of hair. People want to look pleasing, it's only natural.**

(The curtain rises on the inner stage. Gault is standing with her back to the audience, wearing a stylish, hip-clinging dress, with a flower pattern in warm, sensuous colours. She's reflected in triple mirrors)

Gault **How do I look? On reflection?**

Quinn **Pleasing.** *(But he's looking straight ahead)*

Gault **It's not really the sort of thing that I can get away with.**

Quinn **It's perfection.**

Gault **You think it's all right?**

Quinn **Come and choose some scarves.**

(She comes down. The curtain falls on the inner stage)

Gault **How did you talk me into this, Quinn?**

Quinn **Look at these.**

Gault **I don't feel right about it.**

Quinn **She would have wanted them worn.**

Gault **Not by me.**

Quinn Why not by you? You suit them. Down to the ground. Look at this . . . *(He has taken a silk dress off the rack and is holding it up against her)* . . . eh? Eh?

Gault She certainly had dress sense.

Quinn Try it on.

Gault I couldn't take something like this.

Quinn Listen. It's yours if you want it. Go ahead.

Gault Can you unzip me?

(He unzips her and she steps out of the first dress and into the second as they continue talking)

What about Delia?

Quinn She's due home soon.

Gault I meant what will she think about this?

Quinn She thought it was very sensible.

Gault You've discussed it with her?

Quinn She phoned me. *(He finishes zipping her into the second dress)* There you go . . . *(he turns her round)* Magical. *(He kisses her, his hands moving over her body)*

Gault *(Breaking away)* For God's sake, Quinn . . . this whole thing is sick, it's ghoulish.

Quinn It's all right.

Gault I'm not her, you know! You can't make me into her by dressing me up in her frocks!

(Pause)

Quinn I was going to give the most of them to charity.

Gault I'm sorry, that was uncalled-for.

Quinn I just thought, maybe . . . one or two . . .

Gault Of course. And I'm grateful.

Quinn It's not right to leave them hanging like that.

Gault But it must be so painful . . .

Quinn No, no . . .

Gault Seeing them worn . . . it must remind you of her so vividly.

(Pause)

Quinn She was forever at odds with her body, Agnes.

Gault She was very attractive.

Quinn She shrank away from it. There was an element of the angel in her, you see, trapped in her.

Gault What do you mean?

Quinn As if it had flown too low. And some brute creature caught it by the heel. Wrestled it to the ground. Tore its wings. So that it was trapped in the earth. Pining for home. She was always at loggerheads. She rarely wore a new dress for long, two or three times, that's all, they were never a part of her . . .

Gault She always looked so elegant and stylish, when I saw her. Though perhaps a little bit . . . fretful . . .

Quinn Delia wants back.

(Pause. Gault takes the silk dress off)

Gault I don't see how.

Quinn She wants to do the exams. Talk to her at least.

Gault I can't see what possible good . . .

Quinn Just see her. Please.

Gault *(After a moment)* Very well, but she'll have to make an appointment.

(Quinn takes another dress off the rack)

Quinn How about this?

Gault Gorgeous colours.

(He throws it across one of her arms and takes another dress off the rack)

Quinn This one too?

(He throws it across her other arm, takes down another)

And this?

Gault Steady on . . .

(He throws it across her shoulder, takes another)

Quinn This one?

Gault Quinn!

(He throws it across her other shoulder, takes another)

Will you stop it!

(He throws it over her head, she starts laughing, he throws the remaining dresses at her, she runs off laughing, he follows her. Bell comes in stage left to where the dead girl lies on the trolley, carrying a sheet, and pursued by Kane)

Kane Will you knock it off?

Bell I'm not finished.

Kane What do you think a work-to-rule means?

Bell I can't leave her like that, Vincent.

Kane She was brought in like that.

(Bell covers the girl's body with the sheet)

I have to warn you, brother. You're in persistent contravention of union instructions.

Bell Away to hell out of this.

Kane You think I like it? You think I'm a freak?

Bell I sometimes wonder.

Kane Get it into your thick skull! It has to be nasty and it has to be solid. Otherwise all the hardship is squandered.

Bell It's downright callous.

Kane Of course it's bloody callous, it's war. And if you don't have the stomach for it, stay at home and draw your sickness benefit. Because if you go on scabbing like this, old hand, you're going to lose your card.

Bell — The point's already made, Vincent. If the money's there, Quinn'll pay it to us.

Kane — The managements are all together, it's national. Anyway, Quinn's finally lost his magic marbles.

Bell — The strain's definitely showing on him, that's for sure.

Kane — Tranquillised to the eyeballs, I guarantee you. His face doesn't fit right. Not that he ever shows it round here. Who's that?

(The Dean has appeared through the stage left outer door)

Dean — Good afternoon.

Kane — *(Crossing to intercept him)* Hello there, Dean. Mr. Quinn's not in, I'm afraid.

Dean — The place appears remarkably quiet.

Kane — We're just knocking off, in fact.

Dean — At this hour?

Kane — We're involved in industrial action, Dean. Have you not heard?

Dean — Lord save us.

Kane — Mr. Vance is in the building, if you'd like to see him.

Dean — Oh, yes. Thank you, I'll wait.

(Kane and Bell exit. The Dean moves irresolutely towards the desk stage left and pauses there. Delia appears, wearing a black hat and coat and carrying a suitcase)

Delia — Nuncle.

Dean — Is it you, Delia? Are you all right?

Delia — Fading fast, Dean. I'd better not sit down in here or they're liable to embalm me. Where are they all, anyway?

Dean — Apparently on strike.

Delia — What, against the man upstairs?

Dean — Your father, you mean?

Delia — Who art in heaven . . . you know, the sleeping partner. I can't see him negotiating, Dean. His wrestling days are long over. I can't even see him waking up, what do you say?

Dean — Have you spoken to your father yet?

Delia — I'm just this minute off the plane.

Dean — Sit down here and rest yourself. *(He seats her at the desk)* You gave us all an awful fright, running off like that. What possessed you, child?

Delia — I was reconstructing the events leading up to the crime. Retracing my mother's steps, wearing her coat and hat. You should have told me about her, Dean. You did me wrong.

Dean — Your father thought it best to spare you, Delia. He only meant it for your own good.

Delia — A motive which has destroyed whole populations. Besides, it was really himself he was trying to shield. He was able to keep the knowledge of her death at arm's length so long as I was ignorant of it. It couldn't go on for long, though, could it.

Dean Pray God you'll find peace of mind now, the pair of you.

Delia I want to know what you did with her ashes.

Dean Your father scattered them, Delia.

Delia Where?

Dean I'm sure he would rather tell you that himself . . .

Delia It'd cost you less, though, Dean.

(Pause)

Dean Well, now . . . you know how much Agnes loved her garden . . .

Delia In our back garden? He scattered them there?

Dean You have it all now.

Delia He must have done it when I was asleep. Dead of night. By the light of the moon the mad gardener sows his barren ground with ashes . . . you surely must have seen he was cracking up.

Dean Oh no, he'd been most composed the entire time. We had had a service of course at the crematorium.

Delia I visited there last week.

Dean A devil of a place to find, in the middle of that heartless sprawl. It was tragic that Agnes should end her days in such a wilderness. Of course, she wasn't herself, she was oblivious to her predicament.

Delia So why did she lift all the money before disappearing, Dean?

(Pause)

Dean What's that?

Delia She went to London with all the firm's cash reserves stashed in her suitcase, including the borrowed money owed to you. Now, why was that?

(Vance appears)

Vance I'm sorry, I'd no idea you two were here. Welcome home, Miss Quinn.

Delia Thank you, Jonah.

Vance Can I assist you in any way, Dean?

Dean What's that? Oh, there is, yes, I called in to tell you . . . it's Doctor Dempster . . . she died early this morning.

Vance Peacefully, I hope.

Delia Punctually, at any rate.

Dean Oh, she never came out of the coma.

Vance Thank you for letting me know, Dean, I'll attend to it.

Dean What about this strike business, though?

Vance The doctor didn't want a funeral, so it should be quite practicable. I'll arrange for ambulance men to deliver her here. So far as the burial goes, there are still a number of private-sector gravediggers working normally.

Dean — Mr. Quinn might feel that something more auspicious is called for, though.

Vance — The doctor's instructions were clear and definite, Dean.

Dean — Well, my doleful duty's done, so I'll run along. *(To Delia)* Be a good girl now.

Delia — You be a good dean.

Dean — I'm in the running for the Bishopric, you know, so remember me in your prayers. Good day, Vance.

Vance — Good-bye, Dean, and thanks again.

(The Dean exits)

Delia — Nice to see that business is still buoyant.

Vance — How was London?

Delia — If you ever have occasion to mourn, go and tramp the streets of Ponders End for three long winter weeks. It fits the bill. You'll cry yourself dry. Not that you'd ever have occasion to mourn.

Vance — I've missed your sunny disposition, Delia.

Delia — I sat in that grisly crematorium for a whole morning, watching the production line rumble and the furnace doors whirring open and shut. In the country wakes in the olden days, the mourners would get drunk and get up and dance with the corpse. That's the kind of last dance I'd choose. Not jitter-bugging into cinders at the centre of an electric firestorm.

Vance — You think too much.

Delia — In the afternoon I went to a sex cinema. More joyless bodies. The funny thing is, a man trid to feel me up. But that was in the crematorium. In the cinema nobody gave me a second glance. How can you go on doing this, Vance?

Vance — Making a living, that's all.

Delia — Or is making a killing the choicer phrase?

Vance — Give yourself a holiday, accept the world as it is for a spell. Content yourself with what you've got.

Delia — Sleepwalk through life, you mean. I'm working at it, but I'm still inclined to bump into the furniture. Maybe you can steer me.

Vance — At your service.

Delia — Fancy you being sweet on the boss's daughter, what can have caused it?

Vance — One of these days I'll slap that little bum of yours.

Delia — Has Quinn been told of this strike carry-on?

Vance — It's only a work-to-rule, in fact.

Delia Pardon my slang. It's not likely to destroy the business, with luck?

Vance No, but your father's mismanagement might. Far from being buoyant, it's sinking fast.

Delia At last the good news.

Vance Scarcely.

Delia You're not worried about losing your job? A man of your talents and training could always find work . . . in film production, say . . . or party politics . . .

Vance I'm sorry my talents offend you.

Delia It's one thing I've learned from growing up here — there are many forms of dying and many degrees of deadness. I've seen white-haired corpses more alive than you are.

Vance If your notion of being alive is the self-regarding . . . wasteful destructive lunacies of your father and yourself, then I'm happy to remain moribund.

Delia Only you could make 'happy' sound like a swear-word.

Vance I'm getting a little bored at being the butt of everyone's insults.

Delia So that's why you called a strike, I've been wondering. You still haven't told me if Quinn knows about it.

Vance He's been told often enough, but he seems to be wilfully ignoring it. I don't understand what has come over him recently.

Delia You could never understand it. Although it's actually very simple. He's come to grief, that's all. He's finally come to grief. *(She exits. The 'Sleeping Beauty' music is heard. Vance stands, disgruntled for a moment, then he crosses to where the dead girl lies on the trolley. He takes a white gown from a coat-stand and puts it on. Quinn appears, wearing a white gown. Music stops)*

Quinn The purposes of embalming, Vance.

Vance To delay decomposition, thus preventing the leaking of fluids and obnoxious smells. To prevent infection. To restore a life-like appearance.

(Quinn has removed the sheet from the girl's body, and they are fitting a night-gown and quilted dressing-gown to her as he speaks)

Quinn Good. The aim being to eliminate any shocking visual memories. That sort of thing can cause an unnatural revulsion towards passing away.

Vance Unnatural?

Quinn Eh?

Vance Surely a feeling of revulsion towards death is very natural.

Quinn *(Pausing, looking at him sharply)* I'm surprised to hear that coming from you, Vance. That's the sort of superstitious clap-trap the profession has been fighting hard to overcome.

Vance But it's just a fact of human nature . . .

Quinn Concerning revulsion of any kind, it's our job to dispel it. Because that revulsion will not just be directed at the event. That revulsion will be directed at everything connected with the event. Including the funeral director. *(He returns to dressing the girl)* Incidentally, the term 'embalming' should never be used in discussions with a client.

Vance *(Wearily)* I know. Hygienic treatment. Temporary preservation. Taking care of the body.

Quinn Good. Now, today I'm going to deal with Natural Posing. *(He starts combing the girl's hair)*

Vance Before we start on that, Mr. Quinn.

Quinn Well?

Vance How is the firm planning to survive this industrial action?

Quinn Put that out of your head, Mervyn. The profession has never had to cope with that kind of carry-on. Besides . . .

Vance It's into its third week now.

Quinn . . . my boys would never let me down. They all came with me from Fullerton's, you know, every one.

Vance Mr. Quinn, the army is standing by to take over.

Quinn As a matter of fact, old boy Fullerton was raging. He had to close the branch down till he'd trained enough new staff. However. Natural posing. Now, the first thing is to deal with this prior to rigor mortis, right? Pillows.

(Vance lifts two pillows from under the trolley, and Quinn places them under the girl's head)

The aim is for a natural, restful posture. So we try to avoid the old idea of the nose at dead centre and pointing up to heaven. Try to incline the head a bit . . . *(he does so with the girl's)* Prop the chin up. Smooth down the lips into a nice relaxed position – if there's dentures you need to make sure they're properly seated. Now, the eyeballs shrink. So what you need is two wafers of cotton wool spread over them, so as to support the eyelid. Then you can set the eyelids to give the appearance of natural sleep. Coverlet.

(Vance hands him a flower-print coverlet from under the trolley, while Quinn tints the girl's cheeks with rouge. He then spreads the coverlet with the sheet over the girl, turns it down, and lifts the girl's arms out over it)

The arms and hands can be very expressive, Mervyn. The only place they should never be is straight down the sides. There's a host of possibilities . . . one hand folded over the other . . . one over the other's wrist . . . one on the breast, the other straight down . . . or even folded on the breast, that's a favourite with religious people. *(He demonstrates each of these as he goes along)* It's a matter of personal judgement. One thing that can ruin the whole effect, though, is stiff, straight fingers. Bend them to a natural pose – it takes a bit of pressure on the wrist and fingers. *(He does so)* Now. You step back a few paces. To judge the general effect. *(He steps back, surveys the girl. The pose is grotesquely winsome and doll-like)* You see? Magical. Peaceful. Asleep. *(A buzzer is rung off)*

Vance I'll get it. *(He goes)*

Quinn *(Oblivious)* The artistic impulse comes into play here, Mervyn. You can work wonders. It's a creative area. You'll find it repays you to take trouble. Clients are deeply grateful. It reassures them, you see.

(Vance re-appears, carrying trestles, and leading an ambulance man (the Male Employee) and Bell, who are carrying a coffin containing the body of Dr. Dempster)

Vance Through here, please.

Quinn What's this?

Vance Doctor Dempster's remains, Mr. Quinn. From the hospital. Just put it here. *(He has set up the trestles and they place the coffin on them)*

Vance That's fine. Thank you. We're deeply grateful. *(He leads them out again, slipping them money)*

Male Employee & Bell Thank you, sir. Thanks, Mr. Vance.

(Quinn removes the coffin lid)

Quinn Well, Doctor. I suppose they've put you through it. You're not yourself at all. You're looking distinctly unkempt. *(He fetches a quilted dressing gown)* Never worry. We'll soon get you to rights.

(Vance re-appears)

Vance No need for any preparation here, Mr. Quinn.

Quinn Vance, you can take that girl to the Reposing Room now.

Vance Certainly. It's just that the doctor's instructions . . .

Quinn Take care of that for me, please.

Vance Very well. *(He wheels the trolley off. Quinn starts to comb the Doctor's hair)*

Quinn We'll soon have you good as new. Smartly turned out. We're going to do you proud, Doctor. Do the honours. The full works.

Vance *(Re-entering)* Excuse me, Mr. Quinn.

Quinn Eh?

Vance It's just that the doctor did ask for a simple burial.

Quinn The doctor is an old family friend of ours. Vance.

Vance Of course.

Quinn The least of my obligations to her is a decent send-off.

Vance Surely her instructions should be honoured, though.

Quinn Permit me to know the thoughts of my own friends and how they should be honoured.

Vance The doctor was very specific, I gave you the list of her demands . . .

Quinn I've heard quite enough, thank you! You're not in charge here yet!

Vance I'm sorry, I just thought perhaps. . .

Quinn I know very well what you just think, Vance! I know the game you're at behind my back! You just think you can calmly take my business over!

Vance That's not true.

Quinn While I've been treating you like my own son, you've been busy betraying me! I've nourished a viper in my bosom!

Vance You need help, Mr. Quinn.

Quinn Away to hell's gates out of this! I'm sick and tired of your sleekit beady eyes!

Vance Right. *(He pulls off the white gown and flings it aside as he exits. Quinn returns to the Doctor's body. He lifts her up to fit her into the dressing gown)*

Quinn It's only what's fitting, Doctor . . . only fitting . . . ministering to the body's needs . . . you did it for us in life . . . my turn now . . .

(The Doctor grunts with amusement)

No, you can't deny me that now . . . not now at this stage . . . it's a question of proper care . . . professional expertise . . . you and me, Doctor . . . birds of a feather now, eh?

(The Doctor gives a low laugh. Quinn has the gown fitted now and is putting silk pillows behind her head)

. . . all those arguments . . . the plucked flower, you remember that one?

Dempster *(A low murmur)* I'm smiling for you, Quinn.

Quinn A plucked flower . . . you don't throw it on the rubbish tip, now, do you?

Dempster You never saw me smile before.

Quinn You trim it . . . place it in a nice vase, eh? . . .

Dempster It's irresistible when you're dead.

Quinn And is the human body less than a plucked flower? . . . answer me that one, Doctor, eh? *(He begins working on her face)* You never would buy it, though . . . not from a coarse Christian the likes of me . . . unqualified, unlettered, a bit of a common joker, a bit of a joke for a posh girl like Agnes . . .

Dempster — We're both smiling for you now.

Quinn — I could make her smile. . . once upon a time . . . she chose me, Doctor, in spite of all . . . you never cured her of it . . . no cure for the heart, eh? *(Quinn works on at preparing the Doctor's body in a particularly garish way. Meanwhile Vance re-enters, to the desk stage right, followed by Miss Gault)*

Gault — So.

Vance — Here I am.

Gault — As promised. What's this I hear about a strike?

Vance — It's not a full strike yet.

Gault — Well, labour pains anyway.

Vance — More like teething troubles. It's a work-to-rule.

Gault — That must be a nightmare – I mean, presumably people don't die conveniently during business hours.

Vance — The mortuaries are filling up.

Gault — So how do you manage – a skeleton staff, perhaps?

Vance — *(Mock reproach)* Miss Gault.

Gault — Sorry.

Vance — The school's looking very trim.

Gault — I must show you round.

Vance — I've already had a look. It's a curious feeling.

Gault — Remembrance of things past?

Vance — No, how long ago it all seems . . . another incarnation.

Gault — You, of course, developed early, Vance.

Vance — Did I?

(Pause)

Quinn — *(Still working away)* The love was there all right, but it wasn't enough.

Dempster — Your pills are with the receptionist, Quinn.

Quinn — To tell you the truth, I can't help losing heart a bit, Doctor . . . just a little . . . *(He cries quietly as he continues working)*

Gault — How is Mr. Quinn these days?

Vance — Rather out of sorts.

Gault — The news of his wife was tragic.

Vance — I believe she was very gifted.

Gault — Really?

Vance — You must have known her.

Gault — Not personally.

Vance — I imagine her to have been rather like Delia.

Gault — I would guess that Delia takes after her father more.

Vance	Does she?
Gault	In character, I mean. Though she does look like her mother.
Vance	You don't happen to know if there's a history of mental illness in the family?
Gault	Vance!
Vance	None of them seems quite normal.
Gault	They may have their eccentricities . . .
Vance	They're growing more screwball by the hour. *(Pause)*
Quinn	You were heartsore yourself, of course . . . all your life long . . .
Dempster	I'm ready to drink the earth now, Quinn.
Quinn	Don't say that.
Gault	I should think that kind of work would unhinge anyone.
Vance	No more than any other kind.
Gault	It would certainly drive me to drink.
Vance	It's like any other business.
Gault	You're not having second thoughts about the work, then?
Vance	Actually, I think I've just been sacked.
Gault	Sacked? By Quinn?
Vance	He accused me of treachery.
Gault	You must have done some evil deed, Vance.
Vance	I think I've been rather a good boy, on the whole.
Gault	Are you sure?
Vance	Scout's honour. *(Gault gets up, and gazes off)*
Gault	So what now?
Vance	I'll have to see.
Gault	See what?
Vance	What can be done. *(He gets up and moves behind her, gazing off too)*
Gault	Few sights that weigh more heavily on the heart . . . playing fields in February . . . in that failing afternoon light . . .
Vance	Not a soul to be seen anywhere.
Gault	They're all curled up at home by now.
Vance	Sounds inviting. *(He begins to rub his fingertips lightly up and down her back)*
Gault	Stop it, Vance. *(She turns to walk past him but he kisses her. They stagger round a bit together, bumping into the desk, knocking a few things over. Pinned to the desk, she pushes him back)* No! *(Pause)* Not in here.
Vance	Where better? *(They kiss again, pulling each other down. They fall in a tangle out of sight, upstage of the desk. Triumphal music.*

The curtain rises on the inner stage. Standing before the mirrors but facing front is the Dean, now dressed in the full vestments of a Bishop)

Bishop Glory be, John, you can embrace one of the Lord's anointed, the call has come this very minute to say that I've got the Bishopric!

Quinn Dean, is that you I hear?

Bishop Dean no longer, John, it's bishop from here on! Mind you, it was rightfully mine, no question. The man on the spot, the man who's worked his passage. You can be sure of nothing these days, though, it's all politics these days.

Quinn We have to call you Bishop now?

(The Bishop moves down to Quinn's side; the curtain falls on the inner stage)

Bishop You can take your time with the money now, John, I know you've had a hard knock, you may be down but you're not out yet. I won't be hurting for a bob or two. You can pay me back in your own time, when things pick up again.

Quinn No shortage round this way, Dean . . .

Bishop Dean no longer!

Quinn It's all go round here. All in the black. Last year was a miracle.

Bishop I won't sell you out, John, don't worry. We've come through thick and thin together, I'm not going to turn on you now. I know you're a good man, in spite of all. Is that the doctor you have there, isn't it a shame she didn't live to see this day?

Quinn Should have been buried from the cathedral. By rights.

Bishop Wouldn't have it. Strict instructions, you've never heard the like. She would nearly have had us throwing her out in a sack. The mind eaten away with the drink, you see. A sad case. Still — at least we'll pay our respects and give her a proper Christian departure.

Quinn I'm not quite ready for you yet, Bishop.

Bishop Time enough, John. Just you press on. *(He settles down with a newspaper while Quinn works on. Kane appears at the outer door stage left, backing away, as Bell advances on him)*

Kane You're pushing us too far, old hand. You're cutting your own throat.

Bell Let me by.

Kane That's an official picket line out there.

Bell I don't care if it's the Red Army chorus, the old doctor's going to get her funeral.

Kane It'll be your own funeral if you go in there.

Bell Intimidation, is that the idea?

Kane Just face facts. Once you're out of the union, you're out of a job.

Bell Quinn's not going to sack me for doing my day's work.

Kane Wise up. He won't have any choice left if he wants to stay in business.

(Pause. Bell suddenly seizes Kane and holds him in an arm-lock)

Bell I tell you what, Vincent — I'll wrestle you for it.

Kane Quit the high-jinks, this is no joking matter!

Bell Three falls, right? *(He lets Kane go)*

Kane Fucking head case.

Bell Are you ready?

Kane Listen, Albert, this is your last and final chance, now you can't say you haven't been warned . . .

(Bell seizes him in a bear-hug)

Let go, you stupid bloody clown! . . .

(They wrestle round a bit and fall to the ground, Bell gripping Kane in a scissors. Lights full up again on the stage right desk as Gault gets to her feet, smoothing down her dress. Vance also brushes himself off and moves behind her)

Vance Almost dark now.

Gault You're dismissed.

Vance I thought you just were.

Gault Don't start crowing, Vance. You might have been any one of dozens.

Vance Perhaps I have been.

Gault Get out.

Vance That's not very civilised of you.

Gault Don't ever come near here again.

Vance If you say so, miss.

Gault Now scram.

Vance *(As he exits)* Cheers, then. And thank you. You were my very earliest ambition.

(She stays at the desk as the light dims on her. Bell gets up)

Bell That's one.

(Kane tries to run, but Bell grabs him in a neck lock)

Bell Give up?

Kane Drop dead!

Bell Give up? Heh?

(Two mourners — played by the Male and Girl Employees — walk by them, looking askance, and continue through to take their places beside the Doctor's coffin. Bell nods to them as they pass) Good afternoon.

(Kane takes his chance to kick Bell in the shins, and gets free)

Kane That's you done for, Head-the-Ball. You're a dead man now.

Curtains. You stubborn old cunt.
(He exits. Bell dusts himself off and limps into the public room, where Quinn has finished his preparations and removed the white gown. He is at one side of the coffin, the mourners at the other, and the Bishop at the head)

Bishop And why take ye thought for raiment? Consider the lilies of the field, how they grow; they toil not, neither do they spin. And yet I say unto you that Solomon in all his glory was not arrayed like one of these.
(The Doctor laughs)

Quinn Lie still, Doctor.
(The Bishop looks at him in some alarm)

Bishop But friends, what if your lilies are trampled and bruised, what if they're parched and withered? Then they must perforce be tended and nurtured by skilful hands – like the hands of our dear departed sister here today – Lily Dempster. For herself she took no thought, what she should eat, what she should drink *(a shadow crosses his face)*. . . wherewithal she should be clothed. Her thought was always for others – for her late lamented father whom she nursed through a lifetime's illness – and for countless others on whom she bestowed her professional powers of healing. Now she herself is a lily plucked and we gather here to lay her at rest in the good earth. But her memory endures within us as a fresh blossom which will never fade. In the name of the Father and of the Son and of the Holy Ghost, amen.

Mourners Amen.
(Quinn presses his remote control switch and the organ muzak starts. He then leans over and kisses the Doctor. Bell lifts the coffin lid, and he and Quinn fasten it on)

Quinn Where are the other bearers, Albert?

Bell It's on account of the strike, Mr. Quinn.

Quinn Get them in here on the double.

Bell We'll manage fine. *(To the Bishop)* Would you take a lift, Reverend?

Bishop What's that? Oh yes, by all means.

Bell *(Gesturing to the Male Employee)* Sir?
(The Bishop and the mourner take the front of the coffin, Quinn and Bell take the back. They carry it off, with the other mourner walking behind. The organ muzak gets louder, then stops. Delia is discovered at Miss Gault's desk, sitting reading aloud from an exercise book. Gault is standing, listening)

Delia Because we are the tribe which has lost the knowledge of how to die. In the boundless abundance of knowledge by which we act, this supreme skill has somehow been mislaid. Yet this one action – which we all dread – is the only one that's forced upon us all without exception. And we do it in shame and in confusion. Other tribes, who knew much less, at least knew this. They died with conviction and finesse. But we are entirely in the dark. And the black void of our ignorance spreads wider still. For a person begins to die at the moment of birth. So dying is an action that we perform throughout our lives. And so – at the heart's core – we are the tribe which has lost the knowledge of how to live.

(Pause, as Delia closes her exercise book and gives it to Miss Gault)

Gault As usual you write like an angel. And as usual I have only just the foggiest idea of what you're on about.

Delia I tried to say it as baldly as possible.

Gault Yes, but I mean. . . I've always assumed, for example, that death is something that happens to you, not something you do.

Delia Surely killing is what's done to you. Dying is what you do in response.

Gault The distinction doesn't mean a lot to a man who's been hit by a bus.

Delia No, but the form of the killing is a local matter, what I'm trying to say is – the nature of dying is a life-long affair. Personally, I already feel most of the way there.

Gault I do wish you could bring yourself to write about something a trifle cheerier.

Delia This is my last word on the subject, I promise you, Miss Gault.

Gault Thank God. In your case I'd give anything to read about what you did on your summer holidays. *(Pause)* Or in your case, perhaps not. At any rate, you've really been applying yourself, Delia.

Delia Yes.

Gault I'm very pleased about that. You have the ability to do virtually anything you want with your life. Don't let it waste away in bitterness.

Delia I'll try and invent some use for it.

Gault I know the loss of your mother was a bitter blow. . .

Delia I've come to terms with my mother's death. More or less. I only wish my father could.

Gault How is Mr. Quinn?

Delia I wish you'd visit him.

Gault I hope you fully realise, Delia. . . that your father and I. . . you're in no danger of getting me for a stepmother.

Delia It's all right. He just needs company.

Gault He's not ill in any way?

Delia He's bereft.

(Pause)

Gault Well. I'll call in some evening.

Delia Thank you.

Gault This office gets so airless. I can hardly breathe. I'll walk you down to the gate.

(They both stand up)

How are the tap dancing classes?

Delia I gave them up.

Gault I suppose you don't have the time anymore.

Delia I'm a big girl now.

(They exit)

(Kane is entering stage left, removing an overcoat. He looks round with immense satisfaction and then launches into a manic paso doble with his coat for a partner)

(Vance appears through the same door and watches)

Vance Fancy footwork.

Kane Nothing to what went on at the meeting.

Vance Victory, I presume?

Kane Danced rings around them.

Vance That sounds like it calls for a drink.

Kane Too damn right, Mervyn.

(Vance leads the way to the desk)

Vance I shouldn't really be in here.

Kane That circumstance has changed, brother.

Vance How so?

Kane All in due course. Break out that booze.

Vance I knew the Association would cave in eventually.

(He's pouring the sherry and passing a glass to Kane. They sit down and put their feet up on the desk)

Kane Total collapse of stout party. There was a bit of bluster at the start about manning levels. So we obligingly tacked some persiflage on to the basic demands. That was all the face-saver needed. Twenty minutes later they'd conceded everything. Basic rate. Dirty money. Free funerals for members. The lot.

Vance Congratulations.

Kane Including the reinstatement of dismissed brothers, including your good self.

Vance Quinn wasn't there, though?

Kane They phoned him. Apparently he's taking a rest cure. The brother-in-law's in charge for the time being. He wants you to take control of the day-to-day running of the firm in the meantime.

Vance You don't say.

Kane Cheers, Mervyn.

Vance Cheers to you.

(They drink)

Kane You had the right idea. It took the all-out strike to bring them round. If we'd started that way, the whole thing would have been over inside a fortnight.

Vance We'll all have to work flat out to clear the backlog.

Kane I forgot to say. They also agreed to letting Albert Bell go.

Vance Oh yes?

Kane The man was given every chance, but he's too damned head-strong for his own good.

Vance No great loss. He worked at a snail's pace.

Kane Don't I know it. The clients always liked him, though. Listen, this stuff's only fit to put in a trifle, come on out and I'll stand you a real drink.

Vance You're on. *(As he clears off the glasses)* By the way – something I've been meaning to ask you. What was Agnes Quinn like?

Kane Agnes? She was an amateur princess. God rest her. She never had much truck with us mortals. Too smelly by half, that was the impression you got. Speaking of which, just what is the story with Quinn, anyway?

Vance Who knows? Maybe it's glandular.

(They exit. Gong. The curtain rises on the inner stage. Quinn stands dressed in a long Chinese silk dressing gown, over rumpled pyjamas. He is also wearing a wizards's hat, round black joke-spectacles with a pointed nose and moustache attached, and black lipstick. His props are on a small table beside him)

Quinn Hello there, boys and girls, welcome to the wizard's den. There's a friend here with me you should meet.

(He picks up a large wooden cutout figure of a boy)

It's Weepie Willie. What a misery. Blubbering and boo-hooing all the day long, into his hanky. *(He picks up a large handkerchief and holds it over the dummy's face)* One day, though, he cried so hard that he got completely carried away – or at least his head did. *(He suddenly yanks the head off the figure, with the handkerchief wrapped round it)* Never mind, we're all inclined to lose our heads from time to time. We're all inclined to be absent-minded. The only trouble was – Willie's head completely disappeared. *(He spreads the hanky with a flourish: the head is gone)* Well, the doctors didn't like it a bit. He couldn't be allowed out with no head on. So in place of a head they provided him with a nice shiny balloon. *(He attaches an inflated balloon to the figure's neck)* Now, that was all very well, but a balloon can't do too much. It can't pick its nose. It can't hear the sea. It can't smell the ground. So Weepy Willie wished very much that he could get back his head. And he said to himself if only I could get my head back in place, I'd never weep or cry again. And no sooner had he said this to himself — than his wish was granted. *(The balloon bursts and the head is magically restored in place. Quinn picks the figure up and peers closely at it. He walks downstage tinkering with it. The inner-stage curtain stays up. Delia enters)*

Delia — Christ, I thought you'd shot yourself.

Quinn — Where's the sewing machine oil?

Delia — We don't even have a sewing-machine.

Quinn — Willie's spring's all rusty.

Delia — What are you up to?

(He has pushed the figure's head down into the neck; now he presses the catch which makes it spring up again)

Quinn — Just getting ready for the kiddies.

Delia — You mean the party at the children's home?

Quinn — I'm a bit rusty myself, I need to practise.

Delia — Quinn, that was last month.

Quinn — Eh?

Delia — You missed it. You forgot. It's long since over.

(He takes off the hat and spectales)

Quinn — I always do it.

Delia — It's all right.

Quinn — They depend on me.

Delia — They had a film show. You can do your act again next year.

(He pushes the figure's head back down again. Then he sets it aside and slowly buries his face in his hands)

Delia — Let her go, Quinn. Don't fight it. Loosen your grip. It's crippling you. She was what she was. We have to live.

Quinn — *(Removing his hands)* There's a rat in this house, you know..

Delia — You won't listen.

Quinn — The old man's just a bit tired, Dilly.

Delia — Did you take all the pills the doctor left?

Quinn — It was the noise of it that kept me awake.

Deila — What noise?

Quinn — It was scrabbling and scuffling round the place all night, I lay listening to it in the dark.

Delia — You imagined it.

Quinn — No, they're breeding in the garden, there are holes down by the rowan tree.

Delia *(Looking at her watch)* Time I was gone.

Quinn I'll set a trap.

(Knocking from off. Delia goes to answer it)

Vance can manage for a week or two. I think maybe I've caught something. It has me run down.

(Delia re-enters with Albert Bell behind her)

Delia It's Albert to see you.

(Bell goes to Quinn and shakes him gravely by the hand)

Bell I'm very sorry for your trouble, Mr Quinn

Quinn Eh?

(Delia has put on her black coat and hat, and now wheels on a small drinks trolley)

Delia I'm just away. You could offer Albert a drink, father. I'll be late back. Good-night.

Bell Bye-bye, Delia.

(Quinn goes slowly to the drinks trolley)

Quinn You put me in mind of Charlie Crayford, Albert.

Bell How do you mean, Mr. Quinn?

Quinn You're a whiskey man, aren't you?

Bell If you happen to have a bottle of stout. . .

Quinn I'm very sorry for your trouble. . . that was Charlie's meal-ticket. *(He is pouring two whiskies)* Help yourself to water, Albert. You remember Charlie?

Bell Is that the Crayford worked for Fullerton's years ago?

Quinn A little scrawny bird of a man. But a face the length of a wet Sunday. He got the sack in the end.

Bell That's what I came to see you about, boss. . .

Quinn Over-familiarity with the clients, that was the problem. From then on he lived mostly on funeral meats. You remember the grub in those days. The bereaved family was expected to lay on a feast for the mourners, you were judged by it – the amount of food and drink. Charlie Crayford would open his morning paper at the Deaths page. He'd go down the list like a punter with his racing sheet. Pick out a likely-looking prospect – a family in business, say, the father dead, roughly his own age. He'd turn up at the house in his working suit. Take the grieving widow by the hand – 'sorry for your trouble, missus, I knew your husband well many years ago, a finer man never walked the earth'. Always the same act. They'd invite him back from the graveside with the other men and he'd sit down and gravely stuff his face. We'd see him time and time again at the better class of funeral – standing round the fringes, like a shrunken sort of a buzzard. Charlie Crayford.

	One of the most contented men I ever knew. *(He drinks)*
Bell	I got a letter of dismissal, Mr. Quinn.
Quinn	What's that?
Bell	I know it's not your doing.
Quinn	I'm not entirely myself at the moment, Albert.
Bell	If you could just see your way to giving me back my job.
Quinn	I've never been a great man for holidays, you see. Never took one in two whole years. Foolish really. The old engine gets run down, you see.
Bell	I don't like troubling you this way. But I'm in a bad fix, boss. I'd never get another job at my age. If you could maybe just phone Mr. Vance.
Quinn	Another drink, Albert?
Bell	I've worked for you twenty years.
	(Quinn is pouring more drinks)
	I'm the one stuck by you. I'm the one did my job. They should all be getting their cards, not me.
Quinn	Help yourself to water.
Bell	I won't be fobbed off, you made your pile out of me, mister.
	(Quinn drops his glass, smashing it)
Quinn	You don't entirely understand, Albert. The cash flow. The cash flow problem. . . the fact of the matter is, it all flowed away.
Bell	What yarn are you telling me?
Quinn	All flew away. . . flew to London. There's nothing in the till. Don't talk to me about your job. Talk to the banks. The banks own the lot of us. Nothing I can do. There's no virtue left in me, Albert.
	(Pause. Bell stands up)
Bell	You people. I know you for what you are. Oh aye, cuter than a shithouse rat, all right. But you're the real scum of this country.
	(He exits. Quinn slowly covers his face with his hands again, as though trying to hold it together. The light dims on him. Delia is discovered sitting on the steps with Vance, stage left, smoking)
Vance	Your mother just doesn't add up.
Delia	Nobody ever knows the whole sum, that's why.
Vance	What did you find out from your search?
Delia	A lot of the facts. A little of the truth. Which would you prefer to hear?
Vance	I don't know. . . whatever story you're telling yourself at the moment.
Delia	All right. Half-way to the florist's, she decided to write her life

off. She had come to hate it that much. She was a woman without resources.

Vance Apart from being attractive and well-off, you mean.

Delia In a nutshell. Yes.

(Pause)

Vance Go on.

Delia You don't see it because it's so far outside your tiny scheme of things. I know what she felt. You burst upon the world, expecting to astound it with your astounding self. And you don't so much as ruffle the water that your name's written on. On her best days she probably felt like a minor curiosity. The rest of the time it was just a superfluous life.

Vance Why not suicide in that case?

Delia She wanted out of the death factory, not into it. Anyway – reincarnation is a better option. Another town, a new identity, take it all from the top. She cashed in the firm's chips – it was her money anyway – and stepped on to the next plane. She found herself sitting beside a divorced surgeon, a Mr. Wright. He took her home with him. He got her a voluntary job at the hospital, helping out with a redecorating scheme. He died beside her at the wheel of his Rover, on a blind corner.

(Pause)

Vance The only thing I'm inclined to believe is the surgeon's name.

Delia Suit yourself. You did ask.

Vance Does Quinn know all this?

Delia Probably much more. He cremated the pair of them.

Vance When did he find out?

Delia The day after she died.

Vance No wonder he's been indisposed.

Delia You'd better make your peace with him, Vance.

Vance Of course. I'm pretty sure the firm can be brought back into profit, you know – with careful nursing.

Delia The same may not be true of Quinn, however.

Vance What about you?

Delia In the pink.

Vance You've had a lot to cope with.

Delia I'm a hothouse blossom. Forced and lurid. Fading fast.

Vance Growing up.

Delia *(Standing up)* Is that what it's called?

Vance *(Also standing)* I've tried quite hard to disregard you, you know. But you're a bewitching little brat.

(He kisses her lightly)

Delia First the wound and then the kiss. Don't worry, Vance, I'd already decided to indulge you. You're so dependably predictable. I can't foresee any possible way in which you could ever threaten me.

Vance You mustn't flatter me so much.

Delia You're a blessing in disguise, in a crippled sort of way. Come on, let's go home.

(They exit. The lights come up full on Quinn again, still sitting in the stage right armchair, drinking the whiskey. Miss Gault appears)

Gault Are you receiving?

Quinn Eh?

Gault The door was left ajar. I did knock. Perhaps you didn't hear.

Quinn Join me in a drink, Miss Gault.

Gault I won't be staying. How are you keeping?

Quinn I don't drink. As a rule. It's for the rust.

Gault The what?

Quinn Lubrication.

(Pause. She moves about restlessly)

Gault As a matter of fact, I've already drunk my fill this evening. I won't be staying. Just looking in.

Quinn That's kind.

Gault I'm not the brightest of company, however. I'm feeling ever so slightly murderous this evening. *(She moves about again)* There's something radically wrong with me, you see. My secret kink. Courting catastrophe. Flirting with fate. Playing Russian roulette with my entire bloody career. Meaning the only life that I've got. I shouldn't be telling you this, should I?

(Pause)

I was the youngest headmistress, you know, in the country, when I was appointed. It even got into the papers. . . 'Beauty And The Beak'. Highly exhilirating, all that power and prestige. And I owed none of it to anybody but myself. Somewhere down the page, of course, there were also my aspirations as an educationalist. Amazing how soon it all ground down into the present hateful charade. Where's Delia?

Quinn Delia's out tonight.

Gault She's a frightening little witch, your daughter. She has a wonderful gift for provoking the worst from her elders. It was her who made me aware of it – how much I'd been turned into the standard caricature. Bossy, nosey and stiff-backed. Headmistressy. *(She moves about again)* Anyway, I improve the shining hour by dicing with disaster every so often. Last week that little prick Vance came into my office. I let him have it off with me on the floor. For example. Why do you suppose I do it, to prove I'm real? Do I hanker after disgrace and humiliation deep down, do you think? Or is it just profound self-loathing that pricks me on? I hope you're sufficiently shocked by all this. Perhaps it bores you.

(Quinn bends down by the side of his chair and picks up a large rat trap. Dusk has been gradually filling the space)

Quinn — I have to set this trap, it's getting dark.

Gault — I'm going now. *(She moves to the door)* You're the only person I've ever told this to. I hope that somehow strikes you as a compliment.

(She exits. Pause)

Quinn — On account of Agnes being dead, you see. It's a jungle now, that garden. A nest of rats down by the rowan tree. Not that I ever knew one tree from the next, I never looked at trees. Not until she showed me them. It was her creation, that garden. It's a wild jungle now. I haven't set foot in it since she died, except that night, with her ashes, I get a man in with a scythe, every so often, he saw the holes. *(He gets up and moves downstage. It has now grown quite dark)* Because I heard a rat last night. I didn't smell it. I wonder if you really do smell rats, she would have known that, she knew all that, she showed me a world of things. We went into the fields on our wedding day to pick wild flowers for her bouquet. She found a nightshade. 'That's poison!' 'No, it's not, that's not the Deadly sort, that's Enchanter's Nightshade'. I never knew there were different kinds, another was Bittersweet, she showed me it in the hedge. *(He gets down on his knees to load the trap)* I never knew enough, never enough to comprehend her. She kept me forever on approval, she would never entirely give me her blessing. I could hear the sound of her crying from down there, in the summerhouse, for nothing was good enough, nothing free of pain, not with me, not with me, maybe with him, for a spell, but she won't leave me go, won't leave me go. . .

(The inner stage is suddenly flooded with bright light, spilling into the darkened downstage right area as though a light has been switched on in an adjacent hallway. The light silhouettes the figure of a woman in a hat and coat. Simultaneously, Quinn springs the rat trap on his own hand, cries out and reels upstage.) Dear God, Agnes love, will you ever give my head peace! *(He collapses on the floor. The figure of the woman moves down to the stage right wall and switches on a light. It is Delia. Vance follows behind her. The curtain falls on the inner stage.)*

Delia Father! What's that on his hand?

Vance It looks like a trap of some sort.

Delia Get it off.

(Vance prises the trap off while Delia puts her ear to Quinn's chest and feels his brow)

Vance Is there heart failure?

Delia I suppose there is. One way or another. But then again, he never did have a good head for drink. Lift him on to the chair.

(They lift him on to the armchair and recline it so that he is stretched out)

Vance That hand's a mess.

Delia Go and call an ambulance.

(Vance exits. Delia takes her coat off and drapes it over Quinn. She looks at him for a moment)

Delia Looks. Ponders. Hesitates. Is lost. *(She slowly bends over and kisses him. He doesn't stir)* Tries a tentative kiss. Nothing happens. *(She moves downstage)* The prince cleared his throat and shuffled his feet a bit. Did I get the year wrong? he thought. Is this the right address? *(A pool of light is growing on her face as the other lights fade away)* And he thought, it's more like a dungeon, this, than a stately mansion. And he thought, it'll certainly take a lot of redecorating. And he thought, no point in trying to sneak back through that cursed wood. And he thought, what the hell — I suppose after a hundred years of suspended animation, you can't expect miracles. And he said, People really amuse me, though. It's so typical. It's disgusting. It's no joke. It's the living end.

(Blackout. Music: finale from 'The Sleeping Beauty')

END